Home Office Research Study 211

Risk and need assessment in probation services: an evaluation

Peter Raynor and Jocelyn Kynch
University of Wales, Swansea

Colin Roberts and Simon Merrington
Probation Studies Unit, Centre for Criminological Research,
University of Oxford.

Research, Development and Statistics Directorate
Home Office

Home Office Research Studies

The Home Office Research Studies are reports on research undertaken by or on behalf of the Home Office. They cover the range of subjects for which the Home Secretary has responsibility. Titles in the series are listed at the back of this report (copies are available from the address on the back cover). Other publications produced by the Research, Development and Statistics Directorate include Research Findings, the Research Bulletin, Statistical Bulletins and Statistical Papers.

The Research, Development and Statistics Directorate

RDS is part of the Home Office. The Home Office's purpose is to build a safe, just and tolerant society in which the rights and responsibilities of individuals, families and communities are properly balanced and the protection and security of the public are maintained.

RDS is also a part of the Government Statistical Service (GSS). One of the GSS aims is to inform Parliament and the citizen about the state of the nation and provide a window on the work and performance of government, allowing the impact of government policies and actions to be assessed.

Therefore -

Research, Development and Statistics Directorate exists to improve policy making, decision taking and practice in support of the Home Office purpose and aims, to provide the public and Parliament with information necessary for informed debate and to publish information for future use.

"The views expressed in this report are those of the authors, not necessarily those of the Home Office (nor do they reflect Government policy)."

First published 2000
Application for reproduction should be made to the Communications and Development Unit, Room 201, Home Office, 50 Queen Anne's Gate, London SW1H 9AT.

Foreword

It has become increasingly important for probation services to assess offenders attending their services in order to identify effectively their needs, risk of re-offending and any changes in the risk they present to themselves or to others. This report summarises an evaluation, commissioned by the Home Office, of the effectiveness of the two main assessment instruments currently used in probation services in England and Wales. They are Level of Service Inventory–Revised (LSI-R) and Assessment Case management and Evaluation (ACE). This study is also useful in helping to inform the development of OASys, a national joint prison-probation service assessment instrument.

The study examines over 2,000 offenders who were assessed using ACE or LSI-R. The focus is to examine the instruments' ability to predict risk of reconviction, to reliably assess risk and needs of the offender and to measure any changes in these factors over time. The study finds that both assessment instruments are able to predict reconviction at a much higher than chance level and have good reliability. In addition, they are able to measure change in a direction that is comparable with their risk of reconviction. The study concludes that both instruments would be suitable for use within probation services to accurately and reliably assess offenders.

Chris Lewis,
Head of Offenders and Corrections Unit,
Research, Development and Statistics Directorate

Acknowledgements

Many people and organisations have helped to make this study possible. We are particularly grateful to all those who made data available often over inconveniently short timescales, including the probation services involved, the Cognitive Centre Foundation and the Offenders Index section of the Home Office. We are also grateful to Sarmistha Pal, Karen Moreton, Giok Ong, Andrew Roddam and numerous past and present staff of the Research, Development and Statistics Directorate.

Contents

Summary

Aims of the study

This 18-month study was undertaken primarily to evaluate the effectiveness of two assessment instruments which have been widely adopted by probation services in England, Wales, Northern Ireland and the Channel Islands since the mid-1990s. They are the 'Level of Service Inventory – Revised' (LSI-R) and the 'Assessment, Case management and Evaluation' system (ACE). The focus of the study has been on their capacity to assess risk by predicting reconviction, on their reliability as assessments of risks and needs, and on their potential for measuring changes during supervision which are related to changes in the risk of reconviction. The study is also of interest in clarifying the potential contribution of this kind of assessment to probation services generally.

The context of the study

Probation services in the United Kingdom (UK) have been required to undertake risk assessments since 1992, but reliable methods for doing this have been slow to emerge. This problem has become more important as probation services have been required to take on a more explicit 'public protection' function. In addition, probation services need evaluation techniques which will provide reliable measures of change without waiting for the long follow-up periods needed in reconviction studies – in other words, measures which can be applied during supervision and produce results known to be related to the risk of later reconviction. Reconviction predictors based solely on static factors such as sex, age and criminal record (for example the Offender Group Reconviction Scale, OGRS) are not able to do this. The development of effective and evidence-based probation practice has now become a major theme of government policy ('What Works') and this reinforces the need for the kind of assessment and evaluation methods technically capable of supporting such a policy. The Home Office is currently undertaking development work on a new assessment instrument for use in prisons and probation (the Offender Assessment System, OASys) and information from this study may also be of assistance in that work.

The instruments used in this study

LSI-R: The Level of Service Inventory – Revised (LSI-R) is an assessment instrument originally developed in Canada through collaboration between academics, correctional psychologists and probation staff. It is widely used in probation and custodial settings in Canada and is now also in use in other countries including Scotland, and in about 20 probation services in England, Wales and the Channel Islands. It is the product of about 20 years' development, and a considerable amount of research has been carried out on its psychometric properties and its capacity to predict reconviction and various other correctionally-relevant outcomes in North America. Research in England, Wales and the Channel Islands prior to this study had indicated that it could be used by probation officers, that it correlated well with risk as measured by OGRS, that repeated administration could show changes during supervision and that initial assessments were significantly related to reconvictions under supervision in Jersey. What was not known prior to this study was how accurately it would predict reconviction in England and Wales, whether it could measure changes under supervision which were related to changes in subsequent risk of reconviction, and whether it would prove robust in relation to inter-rater reliability and disclosure effects when used by UK probation officers.

ACE: The Assessment, Case management and Evaluation system (ACE) was developed in the mid-1990s through collaboration between the Warwickshire Probation Service and the Probation Studies Unit (PSU) at the Centre for Criminological Research at the University of Oxford. It was originally intended primarily to assist in the evaluation of practice by enabling probation officers to assess the criminogenic needs of offenders in a comprehensive and consistent way, to plan supervision to target appropriate needs, and to use repeated assessments to monitor progress and evaluate how far supervision had been successful in addressing targeted needs. By the time this study began it was in use in about 25 probation areas in England and Northern Ireland, and had been the subject of several local research projects involving collaboration between the PSU and probation services, some of which had led to refinement and improvement of the instrument. The local studies demonstrated its feasibility in use, a significant level of correlation with OGRS scores and a capacity to record changes during supervision. A PSU study in Greater Manchester had also shown a positive impact on the quality of pre-sentence reports when structured assessment tools (particularly ACE and LSI-R) were used. No substantial research had examined the relationship between ACE scores and reconviction until the current study.

Risk/needs assessment derives estimates of the probability of reconviction from a scoring system which includes 'dynamic' risk factors, i.e. risk factors which can change or be changed during supervision. These are equivalent to 'criminogenic needs'. The LSI-R was designed for use as a risk/needs assessment system. ACE was originally designed as an evaluation instrument based on the assessment of needs related to offending, and did not originally produce a risk score. For the purpose of this study, which seeks to evaluate its performance and potential as a risk/needs instrument, the ACE Offending Related Score is treated as a risk score.

The samples

This study is based on initial assessment and reconviction data on 1,115 offenders assessed using ACE and 1,021 offenders assessed using LSI-R before March 1998. Because these are two separate groups of offenders, OGRS2 scores were obtained on all offenders both to control for differences between the groups and to act as an established 'benchmark' risk assessment for comparison with the other assessments.

Risk prediction

Both LSI-R and ACE correlate significantly with OGRS2 scores and provide a range of information about needs. Both also predict reconviction at much better than chance levels: in the LSI-R sample, LSI-R assessments predict correctly in 65.4 per cent of cases compared to 67.1 per cent correct prediction by OGRS2, while in the ACE sample the equivalent figures are 61.5 per cent correct by ACE and 66.4 per cent by OGRS2. Levels of accuracy with women offenders in the sample were similar. The vast majority of items and components in both scales were significantly related to reconviction. Both instruments also predicted serious reconviction and reconviction attracting custodial sentences at better than chance levels, but not well enough to make them appropriate for use as the main method for assessing dangerousness. (Broadly similar results were obtained in these samples from OGRS2.) When assessing the risk of serious or dangerous reconviction these instruments require supplementing with other methods.

Reliability

Inter-rater reliability was measured in relation to both instruments but available data lent themselves to different forms of measurement. In the case of ACE, a study of ten probation officers experienced with the instrument showed that seven out of the ten were consistently quite close in their assessments and only one showed a statistically significant difference from the group. LSI-R was assessed by comparing assessments by different officers assessing the same offender, either on the basis of separate interviews closely spaced in time (25 pairs) or on the basis of shared interviews (10 pairs). Eighty three percent of pairs scored within three points of each other. This suggests that both instruments have an acceptable degree of inter-rater reliability when used by probation officers. Further reliability issues are raised by the possibility of disclosure effects. (Disclosure effects occur when risk scores increase as a result of changes in information about risk factors, rather than changes in the risk factors themselves.) Comparisons of pre-sentence assessments with assessments carried out at the commencement of supervision showed that some problems (particularly drug abuse) were more likely to be disclosed post-sentence, and this was confirmed by a within-area comparison based on a LSI-R using area which changed its assessment stage during the study. Most items showed no disclosure effects. Overall, the effects were small and did not seriously threaten the reliability of the instruments.

Risk-related change measures

When repeated assessments showed increases or decreases in scores during periods of supervision, these were significantly related to higher or lower levels of reconviction. This effect was present to a useful degree with both instruments but slightly greater when ACE was used, probably because ACE currently contains only dynamic risk factors. For example, offenders whose ACE scores increased were over twice as likely to reconvict as those whose scores decreased. The items which changed included some which are very strongly related to reconviction, and it is encouraging to see improvement in these areas during supervision.

Developments in the instruments

There appears to be scope for developing shorter versions without much loss of reliability: for example, a 'Screening Version' of the LSI-R exists which, on the data in this study, appears to predict about as well as the full version. Three options are also explored for improved ACE-based predictors incorporating some static risk factors. Two of these are short versions. Short versions of either instrument are, of course, less comprehensive as need assessments.

Overall

This study indicates that risk/need assessment is a reliable and feasible method for use in UK probation services. The instruments studied can be of significant value in assessing risk of reconviction, in assessing needs and in evaluating the impact of rehabilitative work undertaken by probation services. It is also important to note that both are products of substantial periods of development and refinement, and this appears to be an essential part of the process of producing assessment instruments which are capable of being used effectively.

1 Introduction: Risk and need assessment in probation services

Probation services in England and Wales have only recently begun to use standardised instruments for the assessment of 'risk' and 'need'. Less than a decade ago this practice was almost unknown in the United Kingdom (UK), and its recent growth has been associated particularly with the use of the two instruments which are the focus of this study. The underlying principles are now so widely accepted that the Home Office is developing a comprehensive assessment instrument intended for use in all prisons and probation services (OASys Project Team, 1999) as part of a wider initiative to promote effective practice in services dealing with offenders (Home Office, 1999b). These developments themselves reflect changed perceptions of the role and potential of probation services, and a brief review of recent developments in risk and need assessment is necessary to indicate the context of this research.

The requirement that probation officers should routinely undertake assessments of the 'risk' presented by the offenders with whom they came into contact was first embodied in the National Standards issued in 1992 and repeated with greater emphasis when the Standards were revised in 1995 (Home Office, 1992; 1995). However, there were no widely accepted methods of doing this other than relying on the judgement of individual probation officers. Public protection was increasingly seen as a core task of the Probation Service, particularly as all prisoners serving medium or long sentences were now subject to supervision on release under the provisions of the 1991 Criminal Justice Act. No doubt the Probation Service was to some extent reflecting the wider preoccupation with 'risk' which social scientists (for example Beck, 1992) were identifying as a particular feature of late modern societies, but the Service also had concrete and specific reasons of its own to be concerned about risk as its role in the criminal justice system changed. An inspection of work with potentially dangerous offenders led to considerable concern about how consistently risk assessment was carried out in such cases (Her Majesty's Inspectorate of Probation, 1995) and a considerable amount of development and training activity began to be undertaken around issues of 'risk'.

Much of this activity initially concentrated on raising awareness of risk as an issue in probation services' management and practice, and on conceptual clarification (for example, Kemshall 1996): the term 'risk' is often used to mean both the probability of any reoffending, and the danger of a very harmful violent offence, where the issues of concern will often be the nature of the possible offence and which potential victims are threatened rather than simply the probability of an offence occurring within a given time. This kind of ambiguity about whether 'risk' primarily indicates the probability of further offences or the danger presented should they occur can lead to confusion, for example over what is meant by a 'high risk' offender: is this someone very likely to commit further offences of a routine nature, or someone whose next offence is likely to be serious if it occurs? At the same time Home Office researchers were developing another approach to risk, which was based on using information about offenders' criminal records to provide a quantified estimate of the probability of further offences within a given period (Copas, 1992). This approach was regarded both as a contribution to risk assessment and as an aid to evaluative research, since it allowed researchers to calculate expected reconviction rates for groups of offenders subjected to particular sentences or forms of supervision and to compare these with the rates actually achieved (see, for example, Raynor and Vanstone, 1994; Lloyd et al., 1994).

Other developments in and around probation services in the 1990s also contributed to increasing interest in systematic assessment. One of the most influential texts in the development of effective supervision programmes in the UK was the Canadian meta-analytic research (Andrews et al., 1990) which indicated that the most effective programmes were those which targeted higher rather than lower risk offenders; which addressed needs or problems which contributed to offending, or 'criminogenic' needs; and which achieved a match between programme style and content and the needs and learning styles of offenders ('responsivity'). These three principles of risk, need and responsivity were widely quoted and helped to generate awareness of a need for more systematic assessment of offenders' needs to inform programme content and supervision plans. Evaluation of some probation programmes tended to support the view that better matching of programmes to offenders' needs could help to improve effectiveness (for example, Raynor and Vanstone, 1996). At the same time, the growing interest in effective and evidence-based probation practice led to an interest in methods of measuring the effectiveness of supervision through tests administered at the beginning and end of periods of supervision, rather than waiting typically two or three years for the completion of a reconviction study. This led some services to rely heavily on psychometric tests and psychological expertise to measure intermediate targets of supervision, i. e. targets of change which were believed to contribute to lower offending (for example McGuire et al., 1995) while others were interested particularly in attitudes and problems associated with offending, and a new instrument, CRIME-Pics, was developed for this purpose (Frude et al., 1994). The Home Office itself supported research on a simple 'needs assessment' instrument (Aubrey and Hough, 1997).

All these approaches had specific advantages and disadvantages which contributed to the practice climate in which ACE and LSI-R (the two instruments concerned in this study) became widely adopted. For example, the development of reconviction predictors from a national database of criminal records along the lines initially indicated by Copas' research led eventually to the Offender Group Reconviction Scale (Home Office, 1996) and subsequent revisions: these provide a powerful evaluative tool in reconviction studies and contribute to central monitoring of the effectiveness of criminal justice agencies, but cannot help practitioners to assess needs or to evaluate the impact of supervision, since they include no factors which supervision can alter (in other words, they are based on 'static' or historical characteristics of offenders, not on 'dynamic' factors such as criminogenic needs, which could change). The needs assessment scale evaluated by Aubrey and Hough seemed unreliable for measuring changes during supervision, while CRIME-Pics appeared to be a good measure for some intermediate targets of supervision and significantly related to reconviction, but not very strongly related (Raynor, 1998a). However, a further Home Office study suggested that knowledge of social factors impacting on offenders might slightly improve the accuracy of reconviction predictors based solely on criminal records, which tended to strengthen the case for the inclusion of some dynamic factors in risk prediction (May, 1999). In this context, it was not surprising that some probation services and probation researchers became increasingly interested in the concept of risk prediction based on the assessment of criminogenic needs, or 'risk/need assessment', as already practised in Canada and elsewhere.

Risk/need assessment has been described as a 'third generation' method of risk prediction (Bonta, 1996), with the first generation represented by the individual judgement of practitioners and the second by actuarial methods based solely on static factors such as criminal history. In principle, a well-designed and tested risk/need assessment instrument which incorporates assessment of criminogenic needs into the calculation of a risk score should be able to predict reconviction at much better than chance levels, to help practitioners to target those dynamic risk factors which, if changed, can contribute to a reduction in future offending, and to measure, through repeated administration, whether changes are occurring during supervision which are likely to affect future offending. The potential attractiveness of such approaches, in a Probation Service required to develop evidence-based practice, is readily apparent: however, there was no significant tradition in the UK of developing and working with such assessment methods. This meant that instruments for use in the UK would either need to be new designs requiring a relatively lengthy period of development and testing, or would need to be imported, and would still require re-evaluation and validation in the UK practice context.

This research covers the two major initiatives to date in the development of assessment methods based on criminogenic need in UK probation services. It concerns one 'imported' instrument, the Level of Service Inventory – Revised (LSI-R) (Andrews and Bonta, 1995) and one indigenously developed instrument, the Assessment, Case management and Evaluation system (ACE). This report concentrates on their performance and effectiveness in the Probation Service context in England and Wales; another report by Home Office researchers seeks to address some questions relating to user-friendliness and practitioners' views (Aye-Maung and Hammond, 2000). The next chapter describes the origins and development of the two instruments used in this study.

2   The origins and development of the two instruments

In this chapter we summarise the origins and background of ACE and LSI-R, the two instruments which are the focus of this study. Both arose out of concern for similar issues but with rather different immediate purposes, and there are quite substantial differences between them. The previous chapter identified various purposes of assessment which can be summed up as risk prediction, supervision planning and service evaluation. Whilst all of these are relevant in evaluating the instruments, not all were equally salient in the initial development of each: in particular, the original initiative to develop ACE arose from concerns about service evaluation, while the LSI-R was originally intended to assess the level of risk presented by particular offenders in order to determine the intensity of supervision to which they should be subjected. This chapter summarises, first in relation to ACE then to LSI-R, the developmental pathways which led to the forms of each instrument used in this study. Lists of the items covered by each instrument can be found in Appendix A.

The origins and background of ACE

In 1993 the Warwickshire Probation Committee decided to invite tenders from University researchers to undertake an evaluation of the effectiveness of the work of the Warwickshire Probation Service in the supervision of offenders in the community, either on supervised community sentences or on licences following a custodial sentence. They were particularly concerned to know more about the influence, if any, that one-to-one supervision and group work programmes were having on the subsequent offending behaviour of those offenders being supervised in these ways by probation staff. Ros Burnett and Colin Roberts of the Centre for Criminological Research in the University of Oxford were invited to undertake a feasibility study including a pilot research element in order to determine whether it was possible to establish a system of data collection by probation staff themselves which would provide a valid and reliable basis upon which one could begin to answer questions about the effectiveness of supervision.

The Warwickshire Probation Service thereupon set up the Supervision Practice Development Initiative (SPDI) and included the research project awarded to the Centre for Criminological Research (CCR). A group of 20 probation officers were assigned to work on the research project: from field teams supervising probation orders and combination orders and writing pre-sentence reports (PSR), to a specialist through-care team responsible for work with offenders receiving custodial sentences and including pre-release and post-release supervision in the community, and all staff working in a specialist group work programme unit. It was these staff who worked closely with the university researchers and provided all of the cases during the pilot study.

In 1994 the feasibility study started and the university researchers undertook a literature survey of what existing models for evaluation and data collection had been developed. Also the researchers undertook a literature survey of research findings on criminal careers, the characteristics of persistent offenders, the limited research on desistance factors, and the small but growing evidence on what types of interventions were considered successful in reducing re-offending and levels of reconviction. At the same time the researchers also convened a number of workshops to ascertain from the assigned probation practitioners what they considered, from their experience of working directly with offenders, were the best ways to systematically assess offenders, to document their offending characteristics and their social needs, and to measure changes in individual offenders.

From the outset the aim was to develop and test a system of rigorous on-going data collection which would reflect the existing evidence from international research, but would also be informed by and recognised as valid by the professional practitioners who would have to do the actual data collection. At an early stage it was also agreed that any system should try to include the views of offenders themselves, and their attitudes and perspectives, in a way which could be repeated at future dates. This process of consulting practitioners had an important impact on the design and content of the forms for data collection and in the longer term on the ACE system being used at present. It was also clear from the beginning of the project that it was a total system which was being tested, not simply particular instruments or questionnaires.

The evaluation system used in the pilot study in Warwickshire devised by this process of consultation, consisted of:

- a Core Measures form and an Offender's Views questionnaire (later to be called 'How do you see things going') to be completed at the commencement of supervision (for Probation and Combination Orders) or at the release point for offenders on licences following custodial sentences. The Core Measures form consisted of six sub-sections: criminal career data, social circumstances, substance abuse and addictions, health and mental health, learning ability and personal behavioural characteristics

- a Series of Process Measures forms, used to record information about the process of supervision, including the objectives and methods in Supervision Plans, three-monthly progress on these objectives, attendance, compliance with requirements and subsequent court appearances and reconvictions. These forms were to be completed on a regular basis by probation officers at commencement when supervision plans were prepared, and then at three-monthly intervals to correspond with progress reviews to National Standards.

The number of cases included in the pilot study was 90, consisting of 66 on probation or combination orders and 24 on licence on release from custody, with 74 (82%) males and 16 (18%) females. In all 23 probation officers completed the forms on new commencements between June 1994 and the end of January 1995. Twenty-three other cases which were originally entered as cases for the pilot study were excluded from the final sample for analysis because of the very short periods of supervision, re-arrests and remands in custody, transfers to other areas or revocations in the first month of an order. The average supervision period was 12 months for probation and combination orders, but only four months for YOI and ACR licences on release from custody. Data was only available on reconvictions during supervision periods, and was therefore uneven across the sample, from a minimum of three months to 18 months in a small number of cases. The reconvictions included some for offences which had occurred prior to the commencement of supervision (known as pseudo-reconvictions: these amounted to 8% of all the reconvictions in the sample). A sub-sample (consisting of 31 of the offenders) was interviewed by experienced independent interviewers to ascertain their experiences of supervision under the pilot system. In addition all the probation officers except one and all ten of the Senior Probation Officers (SPO) were interviewed by telephone using a semi-structured interview schedule, at the end of the pilot study, to obtain their views regarding the problems and benefits of the evaluation system in practice, and what changes could be made to improve its potential as an on-going system.

The overall findings (Roberts et al., 1996) were published after the full report of the two-year feasibility study had been received and considered by the Warwickshire Probation Committee, all the senior managers and all the probation staff who had participated in the pilot study. In the analysis of Core Measures and Process Measures it was found that progress in tackling criminogenic problems was much more frequently achieved in cases where the problem had been clearly identified in the supervision plan, and that more specific objectives with clearly identified methods when used, appeared considerably to increase the probability of improvement. When outcomes were related to offenders' risk of reconviction score (using an early version of OGRS) it was found that on average greater improvements in problem reductions occurred for higher than lower risk cases, and from the limited evidence on reconvictions it appeared that the propensity to re-offend in these higher risk cases was reduced to a greater extent than in lower risk cases. The greatest positive changes occurred for high risk male offenders over 21 years of age. The small sample size restricted more precise analysis of what specific supervision practices were associated with the greatest improvements and with what type of offenders.

The staff views of the pilot study were mixed, with 57 per cent in favour of the system and only 9 per cent against it, and a third of probation officers and a quarter of the SPOs neither in favour nor against. The most common complaint concerned the amount of time required to obtain the information and complete the forms. The main recommendation from staff was to continue with the system, but to improve the forms by reducing both their length and the frequency with which they were expected to be used. The majority of staff felt that the Core Measures by the probation officers would be more useful if undertaken at the pre-sentence report (PSR) writing stage of the process.

Following the pilot study report, the Warwickshire Probation Committee decided to award a second contract to the Probation Studies Unit (PSU) in the Centre for Criminological Research at the University of Oxford, to work on the development of the prototype evaluation system. What was required was a fully operative system for use with all offenders on whom PSRs were prepared and who were under supervision by the Warwickshire service, and which could be fully integrated into other recording and data collection systems. This involved modifications to the Core Measures forms, changes to criminal career and offending data collection, and modifications to the process measures and outcome measures including reconvictions. These changes were also fully discussed with a mixed staff group in the service, most of whom had been involved in the pilot study. It was this second version which was given the name ACE: Assessment, Case management and Evaluation, and was copyrighted by the Warwickshire Probation Service and the University of Oxford.

From the evidence of the pilot study it was possible to make limited changes with some confidence. The modifications to the forms were largely to achieve easier usage by practitioners and to facilitate space for narrative evidence to be included, as well as item scorings from zero to three. Warwickshire designed a training programme to equip all staff to use ACE or at least to be aware of its purposes and the reasons for its content and method of administration. No attempt was made at that time to add 'static' predictor factors into ACE, as it was designed to be used alongside the Home Office Offender Group Reconviction Scale (OGRS). In the current study we have used the ACE 'Offending Related Score' as a risk score for comparison with reconvictions, although this does not rule out the development, from data in this study or elsewhere, of differently calculated risk scores derived from ACE. The ACE Offending Related Score is made up of 33 items grouped into 11 components (see below in Chapter 4 of this report, and Appendix A).

Since 1997 ACE has been adopted by 25 probation services in England and Northern Ireland. In Greater Manchester, a small-scale experimental study found that using structured assessment tools (particularly LSI-R and ACE) improved the quality overall of pre-sentence reports by over 20 per cent (Roberts and Robinson, 1998). As well as continued evaluation of ACE data in Warwickshire, the PSU has undertaken studies in Humberside and Northumbria using ACE and LSI-R, and studies of the use of ACE only in the West Midlands, Northamptonshire, Middlesex and Essex. While ACE was initially unique to Warwickshire, it has spread to other services relatively quickly due to two factors: the increasing level of collaboration between services within ACOP regions, and the role of consultancy, training and on going evaluation undertaken by the Probation Studies Unit (Gibbs 1999).

The LSI-R and its introduction to the UK

The LSI-R was developed in Ontario, Canada by two correctional psychologists, Don Andrews and Jim Bonta, both of whom have been significant contributors to the research literature on offending behaviour and on effective practice. Originally entitled the Level of Supervision Inventory, it arose from discussions between Andrews and correctional practitioners, including probation officers, about how to select offenders who required more intensive supervision at a time when caseloads were rising and decisions had to be made about priorities. The designers describe the content of the instrument as having 'three primary sources: the recidivism literature, the professional opinions of probation officers, and a broad social learning perspective on criminal behaviour' (Andrews and Bonta, 1995 p. 1); in other words, the selection of items for the scale was intended to have a theoretical and professional rationale justifying the selection of these particular items as relevant to offending. The theoretical perspective is consistent with that set out in the LSI-R authors' widely-used criminological textbook (Andrews and Bonta, 1994), and a clear concern from the outset was to develop an instrument which would meet the needs of correctional practitioners and support effective rehabilitative practice.

Early development efforts concentrated on testing the instrument through a reconviction study of the first 598 probationers to be assessed (Andrews, 1982); refinement of what was originally a complex instrument to make it more usable by practitioners while retaining validity; and assessments of its effectiveness in other settings such as prisons and 'halfway houses'. The LSI-R manual cites over 20 studies covering thousands of offenders during the 1980s and early 1990s which demonstrate relationships between LSI assessments and a number of correctionally relevant outcomes including reconviction, self-reported offending, parole outcome, breaches of prison rules and violations of supervision requirements. Research has also been carried out to establish the psychometric properties of the instrument in line with American Psychological Association (1985) requirements, and the designers state that 'research data on the LSI-R is now the most extensive of any North American offender classification instrument'. In addition, an independent official meta-analytic study of recidivism predictors in use in North America found the LSI-R to be the most accurate of those studied (Gendreau et al., 1995). A useful summary of research on LSI-R up to the early 1990s is provided by Bonta (1993). Although most of the research up to that time originated from Canada, the LSI-R was also in use in other jurisdictions such as Colorado in the US, and had been evaluated in Victoria, Australia.

By the mid-1990s the instrument had become the Level of Service Inventory – Revised (LSI-R); the change of title from 'supervision' to 'service' was intended to remind users of the rehabilitative purposes behind the assessment process. It was made publicly available, supported by a manual (Andrews and Bonta, 1995), training manuals and training videos demonstrating its application. The materials stressed its rehabilitative aims ('the instrument was designed to assist in the implementation of the least restrictive and least onerous interpretation of a criminal sanction, and to identify dynamic areas of risk/need that may be addressed by programming in order to reduce risk' Andrews and Bonta, 1995). This is an important point about risk/need assessment instruments in general with respect to criticisms of 'actuarial justice' in the criminological literature (for example, Feeley and Simon, 1992; 1994). Such criticisms regard risk assessment in criminal justice principally as a way to determine what levels of coercion and control should be applied to groups of offenders or presumed offenders, often with insufficient regard to principles of natural justice; however, the criticism has less force when instruments are designed and used for rehabilitative purposes (see also Robinson, 1999).

A self-carbonated four-page form (the 'Quikscore' form) was developed with the 54 scale items on the first two pages, and scoring calculated by simple addition on the third page on to which the responses to individual items were automatically copied. The fourth page was reserved for practitioner comments and the recording, where necessary, of decisions to 'override' the case management decisions indicated by the score. The manual indicates the intended uses of the scale, stating that the LSI-R:

- provides a convenient record of factors to be reviewed prior to case classification

- is useful as a quantitative decision aid in case classification

- assists in the appropriate allocation of resources both within and among offices.

Specific criteria are provided by the LSI-R:

- for identifying treatment targets and monitoring offender risk while under supervision and/or treatment services

- for making probation supervision decisions

- for making decisions regarding placement into halfway houses

- for deciding appropriate security level classification within institutions

- for assessing the likelihood of recidivism (Andrews and Bonta, 1995 p 3).

The manual also indicates that LSI-R users should not rely exclusively on it, nor use it as 'a substitute for sound judgement that utilises various sources of information'. Users should be practitioners who 'have an understanding of the basic principles of psychological testing, and especially psychological test interpretation. Although the LSI-R can be easily administered and scored by many different individuals, the ultimate responsibility for interpretation must be assumed by an individual who realises the limitations of such screening and testing procedures'.

Like many psychological tests, the integrity of the instrument was protected by copyright and it was distributed through a commercial publisher, Multi-Health Systems of Toronto.

The introduction of the LSI-R into UK probation services was a result of initiatives taken by the Cognitive Centre Foundation (CCF) in South Wales. CCF is a training and consultancy company working with various clients in the criminal justice sector, and aims to assist in the development of effective practice. Its directors included David Sutton, the former Chief Probation Officer of the Mid Glamorgan Probation Service which had developed links with Canadian correctional psychologists and researchers during the implementation and evaluation of the innovative 'Straight Thinking On Probation' (STOP) programme (see Raynor and Vanstone, 1997). As a result people in and around the CCF had some awareness of LSI-R: for example, an early version of LSI had been used to measure risk levels in experimental and comparison groups in the first probation-based evaluation of the Reasoning and Rehabilitation programme (Ross et al, 1988) from which STOP was derived. Like other bodies concerned with the Probation Service at the time, the CCF was aware of the need for improved risk assessment and evaluation methods and was attracted to the idea of using methods which shared a common theoretical base with the emerging 'what works' literature.

 The research literature concerning the LSI-R, together with the redesigned form and the new manual and training materials, suggested that these could offer an appropriate method for risk/needs assessment in a probation context, subject to feasibility and evaluation studies to determine whether they could be used successfully by UK probation staff and whether the instrument would predict recidivism as successfully here as in Canada. Appropriate agreements were reached with Multi-Health Systems and the instrument's designers to introduce and support it in the UK, and minor modifications were agreed to the questions on education to make them fit the UK system. Discussions were also needed about who could be trained to administer the scale, as correctional services in the UK include fewer psychologically trained staff than in Canada and it was not at first clear whether UK probation officer training could be regarded as equivalent. In 1996 a number of probation services entered into partnership agreements with the CCF to adopt the LSI-R, arranged training for their staff and agreed to participate in pilot studies. These areas were West Glamorgan, Dyfed and Gwent in Wales, Gloucestershire in England and Jersey in the Channel Islands. In addition a number of other probation areas adopted the instrument without becoming involved in full partnership agreements. By 1998, 20 probation areas and a number of Scottish Social Work Departments (which have responsibility for probation and related services in Scotland) were using LSI-R.

The CCF has produced various brochures and reports in relation to LSI-R, including analyses of local data for LSI-R-using services (for example Davies, 1999), while also distributing the reports arising from the independent feasibility study in the pilot areas (Raynor, 1997a; 1997b; 1998b). Briefly, the pilot study has had access to basic data from over 2,500 LSI-R assessments and has found that risk assessments made with LSI-R are consistently and significantly correlated with the same populations' scores on the Offender Group Reconviction Scale (OGRS); this relationship is similar across areas and over time, suggesting that the LSI-R has contributed to standardisation of assessment where it is in use. Repeat testing has shown changes under supervision, with more positive changes in some programmes than in others; needs profiles generated from the dynamic factors in the scale showed basically similar patterns across areas, with some expected variations such as greater problems with employment and money in more deprived areas; and a small follow-up study in Jersey showed LSI-R scores to be strongly predictive of reconviction during probation orders (Raynor, 1998b).

During the early stages of working with the LSI-R in the UK it became clear that the concept of risk/need assessment was fairly new here, and although psychological researchers in the Prison Service had already begun to look at LSI-R as one of a range of possible assessment systems for prisoners (Hollin and Palmer, 1995; Clark, 1998), thinking about risk assessment methods in probation, even among researchers, was largely based on OGRS. Since then, partly as a result of pilot studies and other research involving LSI-R and ACE, the concept has become more familiar. This study aims to throw further light on the potential effects of these approaches to assessment in a UK probation context, and to contribute to the knowledge base underlying future risk/need assessment instruments.

3   The study and the samples

When this study was first proposed, it was designed as an evaluation of what were rapidly becoming the two established instruments for needs-based assessment in UK probation services. It was therefore concerned to discover how effective the two instruments were in estimating the risk of reconviction, and also how they functioned in respect of the measurement of need. Other particular concerns were reliability (would they give consistent results if used by different practitioners?) and disclosure effects (would they appear to show changes which were simply the result of offenders giving different amounts of information at different times?). If reliability were adequate and disclosure effects small or absent, it should also be possible for the instruments to function as risk-related change measures: in other words, repeated assessments should be able to show changes during supervision, and these changes should be related to changes in the risk of reconviction.

At the time this study began, the Home Office was considering the possibility of a common assessment system and had announced an intention to seek tenders in due course. As a result, interim results from this study were required urgently to inform the tendering process and an interim report was produced at the beginning of March 1999 (Raynor et al, 1999). However, by the time the interim report was available a decision had been taken to develop a new risk/need instrument within the Home Office (Home Office, 1999a: this was to become OASys). As a result this report has been given a broader focus, reporting on all the issues mentioned in the previous paragraph but also discussing some developmental issues in improving this type of instrument, and presenting some information about the contribution of different items and components to the risk assessments produced by LSI-R and ACE. This does not necessarily mean that an effective predictor could be constructed simply by lifting effective components out of these instruments: quite apart from any copyright problems which might arise, the way an item performs in a scale depends partly on the design of the whole instrument, on the instructions for its use, on the training given, on its particular definition in the scale, and possibly even its position in relation to other items. All our data are based on the use of items as part of whole instruments, so there is an element of artificiality in isolating them for separate consideration. However, they can throw some light on potential developments in the scales and particularly on the possible effectiveness of shortened versions.

The choice of data for analysis has reflected the tight time-scale of the study. Reconviction data are drawn from the Police National Computer (PNC), which avoids the problem of pseudo-reconvictions (Home Office, 1999c). In order to have cases 'at risk' of reconviction for at least 12 months after assessment, to allow time for reconvictions to register on PNC and for data to be extracted and analysed, we have used cases assessed before March 1998 and therefore drawn from among the first areas in England and Wales to start using each instrument: Dyfed, Gloucestershire, Gwent and West Glamorgan for LSI-R and Humberside, Northumbria and Warwickshire for ACE. These areas have different characteristics and produce slightly different samples of offenders (see Table 3.1 below). We therefore make extensive use of a new form of OGRS (OGRS2) in the analysis, both to control for differences between the samples and as a 'benchmark' risk predictor validated for England and Wales, to assess the performance of the other measures. OGRS2 scores were calculated for us from the Offenders Index (OI): see Home Office, 1999c. As OGRS2 is designed to predict OI reconvictions within two years and our reconviction data are based on PNC reconvictions within one year, some problems of comparability needed to be overcome, as explained in Chapter 4.

Table 3.1: *Demographic, stage-of-assessment and Index Offence sentence profiles of the LSI-R and ACE cases at first assessment*

	LSI-R		ACE	
Number of cases	1,021		1,186	
Area totals:	Dyfed	34	Humberside	198
	Gloucestershire	529	Warwickshire	668
	Gwent	312	Northumbria	320
	West Glamorgan	146		
Age: average in years (sd)	27.4 years (8.9)		27.4 years (9.4)	
% 16-20 years	25		27	
% 21-25 years	27		25	
% 26-30 years	19		19	
% > 30 years	30		28	
	N	%	N	%
Sex: Male	845	83	1048	88
Female	176	17	138	12
Stage of first assessment:	N=1,021	%	N=1,186	%
Pre-sentence report	874	86	970	82
Commencement	147	14	120	10
Post release	0	0	96	8
Type of Sentence on Index Offence (PNC):	N=973	%	N=964	%
Probation	382	39	322	33
Community service	321	33	289	30
Custody	95	10	175	18
Other	175	18	178	19
Race (PNC codes)	N=793	%	N=964	%
White European	760	96	904	94
Afro-Caribbean	18	2	19	2
Asian	4	1	21	2
Other	1	0	-	
Unknown	10	13	20	2

Sources: OI data (all demographic, sentence), Probation (stage of assessment) and LSI-R/ACE assessment forms.

Another difference between the samples affects the comprehensiveness of some of the information: in the ACE-using areas in the study, assessments were fully entered on computer records at the time they were made, whereas the LSI-R cases were drawn from areas which kept central records mainly of total scores, so that information on items and components had to be recovered by the research team from copies of paper 'Quikscore' forms. These were often not held centrally and could not always be located easily by the probation services concerned, with the result that information on components is missing for a number of the LSI-R cases.

Restrictions were placed on the number of cases which could be followed up for reconviction analysis, owing to high demand on the Offenders Index section of the Home Office. Also a substantial number of cases (particularly cases involving LSI-R) which were included in the reconviction searches had to be excluded from subsequent analysis because the matching of data to cases was considered not fully reliable. However, analysis of the unmatched cases shows that they do not differ significantly from the matched cases in respect of variables likely to affect reconviction such as age and sex, and they are drawn from all the geographical areas in the study, so they are unlikely to distort the overall results. The eventual number of cases, as summarised in Table 3.2, was 2,136, rather less than three times the number included in the interim report, which covered 812 cases. For this reason and in response to problems of missing data, the total (N) of cases varies somewhat from table to table, as we have in each case sought to include in the analysis all cases in which the information relevant to that table was available.

Table 3.2: ACE and LSI-R sample size

	LSI-R		ACE	
	first assessment	second assessment	first assessment	second assessment
OGRS and reconviction data	948	171	903	163
OGRS data only	-	-	60	5
Reconviction data only	73	16	61	10
Unmatched cases	507	-	162	25
Total cases submitted	1,528	187	1,186	203

The remaining chapters of this report summarise our findings in relation to risk prediction and reconviction; reliability and disclosure effects; risk-related change measurement; possible further developments in the instruments, and finally the implications for the feasibility and prospects of risk/need assessment in probation services. The appendices present some further more detailed material relating to individual scale items, regression analyses, and the conversion of LSI-R and ACE scores into probabilities of reconviction.

4   Risk prediction, risk factors and reconviction

Risk and need profiles in each sample, and their relationship to OGRS2

The LSI-R and ACE approaches to need and risk assessment have similarities in relation to the range of 'dynamic' items used in both, but also important differences in the way each estimates the probability of re-offending as measured by reconviction. In LSI-R, the assessment of needs and risk are interwoven as the LSI-R 'risk' score is derived from both the 'needs' items and the 'static' criminal history variables; whereas in ACE, only 'dynamic' needs variables are rated for the ORS (Offending Related Scores).

Table 4.1 shows the distribution of 'risk scores' in each sample using the risk bands normally used with each instrument (and therefore not directly comparable with each other). (For LSI-R bands see Raynor, 1998b; the ACE bands have been newly calculated in the light of data collected for this study). Figure 4.1 shows the distribution of scores, both approximating to a normal distribution but with some skewing. Among the ACE cases there is a small number of offenders with very high ORS scores.

Table 4.1:   Total scores of first assessment LSI-R and ACE cases

LSI-R	(LSI-R N=1,021)		ACE	(ACE N=1,186)	
Mean (sd)	20.1	(9.7)	mean(sd)	21.1	(12.9)
'Risk':	N	%	'Risk' score bands:	N	%
Low risk 0-10	189	18	Low 0-8	214	18
Moderate risk 11-25	518	51	Low/medium 9-15	242	20
High risk 26-35	255	25	Medium 16-26	362	31
Very high risk 36 +	59	6	Medium/high 27-39	244	21
			High 40+	124	11

Figure 4.1: Histograms of LSI-R scores and ACE offending-related scores

LSI-R risk/needs scores

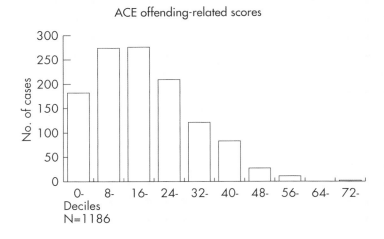

ACE offending-related scores

To examine how the components of LSI-R and ACE (in other words the main indicators of criminogenic need) were distributed in each sample, the proportion of each sample scoring in a particular risk component was expressed as a proportion of the maximum possible score for that component within the sample. This is a technique developed by the Cognitive Centre for reporting to probation areas on needs profiles revealed by LSI-R (see, for example, Davies, 1999) and it partly overcomes some of the problems of comparability arising from differences in instrument design; however, these cannot be completely overcome. The results of this analysis are presented in Table 4.2 for ACE and table 4.3 for LSI-R.

Table 4.2: **Percentage of first assessment ACE cases who had 'risk/needs' factors**
N=1,186

Component	Offending-related risk/needs as % of maximum
Accommodation and neighbourhood	16
Employment, training and education	28
Finances	32
Family/personal relationships	26
Substance abuse and addictions	16
Health	12
Personal skills	23
Individual characteristics	17
Lifestyle and associates	36
Attitudes	21
Motivation	16

ACE: Risk/needs factors are defined as offending-related scores (ORS) for each item. These are reduced to binary (see appendix), and calculated as the percentage of the maximum possible for each component.

In comparing these figures with Table 4.3, it should be borne in mind that they are not strictly comparable and indeed it is probable that the two samples of offenders are rather more similar than these figures would suggest. The lower numbers in the LSI-R table reflect the difficulty of collecting full information on LSI-R components.

Further information on the frequency of scoring in relation to individual scale items can be found in Appendix A; again this information should be interpreted cautiously, owing to the difficulty of assigning an exact meaning to an individual item when abstracted from the instrument of which it forms a part.

Table 4.3: **Percentage of first assessment LSI-R cases who had 'risk/needs' factors**
N=805

Component/risk factor	Criminogenic risk/needs as % of maximum
Criminal history	40
Unemployment	71
Education	43
Financial	62
Family/marital	31
Accommodation	22
Leisure/recreation	59
Companions	43
Drugs/alcohol	37
Alcohol only	39
Drugs only	34
Emotional/personal	18
Attitudes/orientation	20

Notes: Missing values are excluded from percentage calculations.
LSI-R: Items are recorded as binary in LSI-R scoring. The sum of relevant item scores is expressed as the percentage of the maximum possible for each component or risk factor.

Table 4.4 shows the relationship between LSI-R scores, ACE offending-related scores (ORS) and OGRS2 scores in each sample. Both ACE and LSI-R correlate significantly with OGRS2, though the correlation is closer for LSI-R. The Pearson correlation for LSI-R and OGRS2 is within the range reported in Raynor, 1998b; the ACE:OGRS2 Pearson correlation is fairly high compared to those recorded in other studies of ACE. Table 4.5 repeats this analysis for women offenders only: the numbers are fairly small but the correlations continue to be significant and positive.

Table 4.4: Correlation of LSI-R and ACE total risk scores with OGRS2 scores (all cases)

	Average (mean)	SD	Coefficient (Pearson)	Significance of correlation with OGRS2
LSI-R N=948	20.17	9.64	.520	.000
OGRS (LSI-R cases)	49.92	27.82		
ACE ORS N=963	21.49	12.97	.428	.000
OGRS (ACE cases)	50.59	27.66		

Significance test: Pearson's correlation

Table 4.5: Correlation of LSI-R and ACE total risk scores with OGRS2 (women only)

	Average (mean)	SD	Coefficient (Pearson)	Significance of correlation with OGRS2
LSI-R N=163	21.17	9.15	.385	.000
OGRS (LSI-R cases)	34.14	23.97		
ACE ORS N=105	20.84	12.98	.523	.000
OGRS (ACE cases)	34.42	23.96		

Significance test: Pearson's correlation

Overall risk scores and reconvictions

Table 4.6 shows the overall numbers and proportions of each group reconvicted within 12 months, according to PNC records, and also the numbers and proportion of those reconvicted for 'more serious' offences and for offences which attracted a custodial sentence. The Home Office uses an eight-point scale to classify the seriousness of standard list offences: this runs from A (most serious) to H. The classification is based mainly on the maximum penalty available, with some adjustment to reflect the percentage use of custody in a 1994 sample of sentences. Category D offences usually carry a maximum penalty of 14 years' imprisonment; categories A-C carry more severe maximum penalties, including life imprisonment. 'More serious' offences in this study are those in categories A-D, which include most violent and sexual offences.

Table 4.6: Reconvictions among the LSI-R and ACE cases

	LSI-R		ACE	
Total N	1,021		964	
	N	%	N	%
Not reconvicted	601	58.9	562	58.3
Reconvicted	420	41.1	402	41.7

Source: PNC

'More serious' reconvictions among the LSI-R and ACE cases

	LSI-R		ACE	
Total N	902		964	
	N	%	N	%
No/'less serious' reconviction	854	94.7	908	94.2
'More serious' reconviction	48	5.3	56	5.8

'More serious' offences are those in Home Office categories A-D; 'less serious' offences are those in Home Office categories E-H.
Source: PNC, Home Office 'seriousness' classification (A-H).

Reconvictions resulting in custody among the LSI-R and ACE cases

	LSI-R		ACE	
Total N	1,007		964	
	N	%	N	%
No/non-custodial reconviction	929	92.3	873	90.6
Custodial reconviction	78	7.7	91	9.4

Source: PNC

In order to arrive at a straightforward measure of how well the instruments were estimating risk, we adopted the 'per cent correctly predicted' procedure described by Copas (1992) and used by May in his recent study of social variables and reconviction (May, 1999). Basically this involves taking the range of predictor values yielded by a sample, dividing them into 'high' and 'low' at a point corresponding to the proportions actually reconvicted or not reconvicted, then treating all 'high' scores as predicting reconviction and all 'low' scores as predicting non-reconviction. Reconvicted high scorers and non-reconvicted low scorers are then counted as 'correct' predictions. For reasons explained by Copas (1992), the proportion correctly predicted cannot normally exceed 75 per cent even for an optimally effective predictor if the actual reconviction rate is 50 per cent, which is close to the reconviction rate observed in our sample. (For example, Copas' own predictor, from which OGRS was eventually developed, yielded 67.4% correctly predicted in the construction sample and 66.6% in the validation sample. Tossing a coin, which is a form of random prediction, would be expected to yield 50% correct.)

In order to provide some control for differences between the samples, OGRS2 scores were used; however, the basic OGRS2 prediction is not directly relevant, as it gives the probability of an Offender Index offence within two years rather than a PNC offence within one. Instead the OGRS2 score has been treated as another risk measure and subjected to the same '% correctly predicted' analysis as the ACE and LSI-R scores. Table 4.7 shows the results. (It should also be noted that the limitations of the relatively simple and straightforward '% correctly predicted' method mean that it is useful to supplement it with other methods of analysis: for examples, see Figure 4.2 and Table 4.12 below. The results produced by the simple '% correctly predicted' calculation are very similar to those produced by logistic regression in Table 4.12)

Table 4.7: **Differences in first assessment scores (LSI-R, ACE and OGRS2) between cases which are reconvicted and not reconvicted over a 12-month period: all cases (men and women)**

Score type	Not reconvicted		Reconvicted		Signif	% correctly predicted	% false neg
	Mean	(sd)	Mean	(sd)	t-test		
LSI cases							
N= 948	N=546		N=402				
LSI-R	17.25	(9.11)	24.13	(8.92)	.000	65.4***	16.5
OGRS2	40.56	(26.13)	62.64	(24.86)	.000	67.1***	15.5
ACE cases							
N= 903	N=510		N=393				
ACE ORS	18.34	(11.61)	25.46	(13.39)	.000	61.5***	19.2
OGRS2	41.79	(25.95)	62.07	(25.61)	.000	66.4***	16.7

chi-square levels of significance ***<.001; ** <.01; * <.05.
Method: Copas method (see text).

It is clear that all three instruments predicted reconviction at much better than chance levels. The most effective was OGRS2, closely followed by LSI-R and then by ACE. These results are consistent with those found at the interim report stage, except that the current revised version of OGRS (OGRS2) appears to be a more effective predictor than the version in use at that time. (For a more comprehensive assessment of the revised OGRS based on a much larger sample, see Taylor, 1999). The more accurate predictors also produce lower proportions of false negatives, i.e. people expected not to reconvict who actually do reconvict. This measure is arguably relevant to public safety. Figure 4.2 supplements the '% correctly predicted' measure by showing that the relationship between predicted and actual outcomes holds quite well across the full range of scoring (see Appendix D of Lloyd at al., 1994 for a discussion of the methodological point).

Figure 4.2:   Reconviction rates for LSI-R and ACE ORS compared with OGRS2

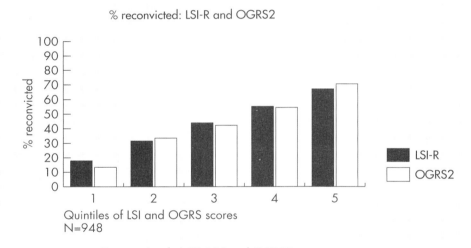

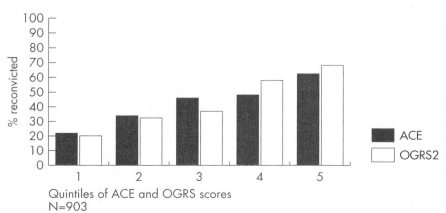

Table 4.8 repeats the analysis for women offenders only and, in spite of the fairly small numbers of women in the samples and their lower reconviction rate, the results are broadly consistent with Table 4.7.

Table 4.8: ***Differences in first assessment scores (LSI-R, ACE and OGRS2) between cases which are reconvicted and not reconvicted over a 12-month period: women only***

Score type	Not reconvicted		Reconvicted		Signif	% correctly predicted	% false neg
	Mean	(sd)	Mean	(sd)	t-test		
LSI cases							
N=163	N=106		N=57				
LSI-R	18.92	(8.26)	25.35	(9.31)	.000	65.0**	16.6
OGRS2	28.14	(21.41)	45.28	(24.66)	.000	66.9**	16.6
ACE cases							
N= 101	N=67		N=34				
ACE ORS	19.22	(12.19)	23.74	(13.40)	.092	60.4ns	19.8
OGRS2	29.82	(21.15)	44.41	(25.93)	.003	68.3**	15.8

** significance <.01   ns = not significant

Tables 4.9 and 4.10 apply a similar analysis to the question of whether the various instruments help to predict 'serious' reconviction, and reconviction attracting a custodial sentence (which can be regarded as a measure of 'seriousness' as perceived by sentencers). In these cases, as only small minorities reconvict seriously, we indicate not only what proportion of 'positives' were correctly predicted but also what proportion were not. The reason for this is that it is quite possible for an outcome which applies to a small minority to be more probable at higher levels of the predictor score, but because such a small proportion of scores fall in the band that notionally 'predicts' that outcome, the actual number of cases with that outcome is greater among the larger pool of cases with predictor scores below the threshold. (This resembles the well-known demographic argument that while it is possible to identify areas where most of the population is poor, the majority of poor people actually live outside those areas, forming a smaller proportion of a much larger population and therefore exceeding in number the inhabitants of the 'poor' areas.)

The tables show that something like this does happen: all the predictors function in such a way that serious outcomes are significantly more likely among very high scorers, but the majority of the serious outcomes actually fall outside the highest scoring group (for example, of the 46 seriously reconvicted LSI-R cases, the majority are not among the 46 highest scorers, even though the 46 highest scorers are more likely to reconvict seriously than the 788 lower scorers).

These results suggest that it would be unwise to rely on any of these instruments as the sole source of risk assessment in relation to serious offences (see also Vennard and Hedderman, 1999; Taylor, 1999). A separate 'dangerousness' assessment is needed based on an analysis of past dangerous behaviour and current risk factors, and while this assessment might be triggered by high scores on a risk/need instrument, that should not be the only trigger. Others might be current or previous violent behaviour, or positive responses to particular items in assessment scales. Similar comments might be made about the prediction of custodial outcome: this clearly reflects factors other than criminogenic need, such as the nature of the current offence and the length of the offending history.

Table 4.9: Differences in first assessment scores (LSI-R, ACE and OGRS2) between cases which are reconvicted of 'more serious' offences and cases not reconvicted or reconvicted of 'less serious' offences over a 12-month period

Score type	No/'less serious' reconviction		'More serious' reconviction		Sign.	'Serious' threshold[1]	% positives which were correctly predicted	% positives which were not predicted	% total which were false negatives
	Mean	(sd)	Mean	(sd)	t-test	Score	%	%	%
LSI cases									
N= 834	N=788		N=46						
LSI-R	19.50	(9.63)	25.30	(8.94)	.000	36	8.7	91.3	5.0
OGRS2	50.81	(26.58)	67.91	(24.11)	.000	92	30.4	69.6	3.8
ACE cases									
N= 903	N=847		N=56						
ACE ORS	21.12	(12.84)	26.29	(13.09)	.004	44	8.9	91.1	5.6
OGRS2	49.61	(27.59)	65.86	(24.66)	.000	92	8.9	91.1	5.6

1   'Serious threshold' is the score at or above which the instrument 'predicts' that reconviction will be for a 'more serious' offence (i.e., in categories 'A-D').

Table 4.10: Differences in first assessment scores (LSI-R, ACE and OGRS2) between cases with reconvictions resulting in custodial sentences and others over a 12-month period

Score type	No/non-custodial reconviction		Custodial reconviction		Sign.	Custodial threshold[1] Sign.	% positives which were correctly predicted	% positives which were not predicted	% total which were false negatives
	Mean	(sd)	Mean	(sd)	t-test				
LSI cases									
N= 934	N=859		N=75						
LSI-R	19.65	(9.59)	26.35	(8.15)	.000	34	21.3	78.7	6.3
OGRS2	48.22	(27.56)	68.64	(23.99)	.000	90	24.0	76.0	6.1
ACE cases									
N= 903	N=814		N=89						
ACE ORS	20.90	(12.82)	26.33	(12.74)	.000	41	14.6	85.4	8.4
OGRS2	48.40	(27.13)	70.91	(24.36)	.000	89	31.5	68.5	6.8

Source: Offenders Index (OGRS2) calculations; PNC (reconviction); LSI-R and ACE data.

Scale components and reconvictions

The ACE and LSI-R total scores are made up from a number of components which are included because they measure a criminogenic factor. Table 4.11 shows how the component scores of each scale were differently distributed between those reconvicted and those not reconvicted of any standard list offence. In both scales, all components appear to discriminate significantly between those reconvicted and those not reconvicted (shown in column 2), with the exceptions of 'family and personal relationships' and 'health' in ACE and 'emotional/personal' in LSI-R. (The relationship of individual items to reconviction can be found in Appendix A.) In both scales, the components which relate to mental health ('health' in ACE and 'emotional/personal' in LSI-R) do not discriminate between those reconvicted and those not reconvicted. This may be due to variability of expertise in psychological assessment within the Probation Service.

The analysis indicates that a higher total ACE or LSI-R score and most higher component scores are predictive of reconviction. However, some of the risk scores measure factors which overlap to some degree. For example, offenders who are unemployed or have financial problems are more likely to be engaged with the benefits system or to have less security of accommodation. Therefore, the risks of reconviction for such offenders may relate to one or more component (or item) concerned with employment, finances or accommodation.

Table 4.11: Difference between offending-related scores for those reconvicted/not reconvicted (12-month follow-up)

a) ACE

Component	Significance of difference of means between those reconvicted versus not reconvicted (12-month)	
	Unadjusted significance	Adjusted level of significance
Accommodation	.000	***
Employment/education	.000	***
Finances	.000	***
Family/personal relationships	.156	
Substance abuse	.000	***
Health	.291	
Personal skills	.001	*
Individual characteristics	.000	***
Lifestyle and associates	.000	***
Attitudes	.000	***
Motivation	.000	***
TOTAL SCORE	.000	***
N		964

b) LSI-R

Criminal history	.000	***
Education/employment	.000	***
Financial	.000	***
Family/marital	.000	**
Accommodation	.000	***
Leisure/recreation	.000	***
Companions	.000	***
Alcohol/drug problem	.000	***
Emotional/personal	.771	
Attitudes/orientation	.000	***
TOTAL SCORE	.000	***
N		790

Independent samples t-tests: Levels of significance of t-statistic (adjusted for the multiple t-tests):
* adjusted significance < .05; ** adjusted significance < .01; *** adjusted significance < .001

Multivariate analysis is required to isolate the importance of any one particular component or item of the scale in the risk of reconviction. Logistic regression was used to highlight the independent effect of the total score, static and dynamic scores, and components or items of each scale. (Our procedures differ in some respects from those adopted by May 1999, in order to arrive at a clearer measure of the relative contribution of static and dynamic factors.)

Table 4.12 shows the scores (total, component or item) associated with increased risk of reconviction for each model, with the results for ACE models in Table 4.12a and for LSI-R models in Table 4.12b. In the table, the scores are ranked by the change in odds of reconviction associated with one unit change in the score (that is, the odds ratio), and the asterisks indicate confidence that the odds increase with a higher score. The models are identified by the numbers in brackets in the column headings. (The complete lists of variables included in each model and statistical results of the logistic regressions are in Appendix B.) The main findings from the logistic regression are summarised after the table.

Table 4.12: Factors related to an increased risk of reconviction (12 months): results from different models of static and dynamic criminogenic factors and area

a) ACE models

	Single factor (1)		Static and dynamic factors (2)	Comp-onents (3)	Items (4)
	ACE	OGRS2			
Total ACE ORS score	***		***		
OGRS2		***	***		
ORS Components:					
Substance abuse				**	
Lifestyle				***	
Attitudes				**	
Items:					
(thinks reoffending inevitable)					***
(associates cause risk)					**
(drugs)					**
(impulsiveness)					**
% correctly predicted	61.2	67.2	66.9	64.0	64.6
Pseudo R^2	.099	.172	.195	.138	.174

b) LSI-R models

	Single factor (1)		Static and dynamic factors (2)	Comp-onents (3)	Items (4)
	LSI-R	OGRS2			
Total LSI-R score	***				
LSI-R dynamic score			***		
OGRS2		***	***		
LSI-R components:					
Financial				***	
Companions				***	
Criminal history				***	
Items (LSI-R):					
(no continuous employment)					*
(financial problems)					*
(low fixed income)					*
(criminal acquaintances)					*
(arrested under age 16)					*
Area			*	*	*
% correctly predicted	65.8	67.9	69.7	69.3	72.7
Pseudo R^2	.164	.200	.271	.218	.323

'% correctly predicted' is different from that reported in Table 4.4 because it is the classification from the regression using a cut off of 0.5, and not identical to that derived by the Copas method.
The 'pseudo R^2' (Nagelkerke R^2) is analogous to R^2 in multiple regression.

The main findings from the logistic regression analysis were as follows.

- *Static versus dynamic total scores (single factor and static/dynamic models)* An increase in ACE ORS (dynamic) and LSI-R (static/dynamic) *total scores* is associated with an increased risk of reconviction (Model 1). Our results suggest that the increased risk of reconviction associated with the dynamic scores is greater than that associated with static scores (OGRS2) (see ranking of items in Model 2 of table 4.12). However, the explanatory value of the model (pseudo R^2) is increased by the inclusion of static scores.

- *Independent effect of static criminal history component (LSI-R component model)* LSI-R components include criminal history: this independently increases risk of reconviction, but less than the independent effect of dynamic components (see ranking in Model 3).

- *Independent effects of components and items (component and item models)* The component and item models for ACE and LSI-R confirm the multi-dimensionality of the risk of reconviction. For ACE (but not LSI-R), these models are the first multivariant analysis of risk of reconviction for the instrument, and therefore invite further testing of reliability and validity. The LSI-R models are broadly in line with published multivariant analyses of risk of reconviction (summarised in Andrews and Bonta, 1995) and also suggest limits on the generalisability of results. Finances/employment, companions and criminal history significantly increase the risk of reconviction in all areas. Sub-groups of offenders with particular risk factors are taken into account in the area variable.

- *ACE component and item models* Within the ACE sample, an increased risk of reconviction is associated with components related to an offender's lifestyle (substance abuse, lifestyle and associates) and attitudes.

- *LSI-R component and item models* Within the LSI-R sample, an increased risk of reconviction is associated with components related to finances, companions and criminal history. This result is robust to different constructions of components which remove the effects of routing (for example, a positive score on the item 'some criminal friends' necessarily scores on 'some criminal acquaintances'). The item model for LSI-R includes items which increase the risk of reconviction from four components: finances, companions, criminal history and employment. Within LSI-R, inter-component correlation of the items is small except for employment and finances, which are highly correlated because of the interlinking of unemployment and benefits rules.

- *External influences (area and sex)* Inclusion of area in the component and item models provided a control for any variation in the use of the instrument and regional influences (such as area-based sub-groups of offenders, or special regional differences). Area was not an independent influence in the ACE models. One of the LSI-R areas believed that its quality assurance procedures relating to the use of the instrument needed to be improved, and another was carrying out first assessments only at the commencement stage rather than for the pre-sentence report (see section on disclosure effects in Chapter 5). Furthermore, the inclusion of area within models allowed us to control for regional dynamic contexts such as prevalence of low income or accommodation problems. Sex was not an independent influence on risk in either the ACE or LSI-R samples.

The component and item models' '% correctly predicted' and explanatory value should be treated with caution. The models do, in fact, fit some cases very poorly, especially the item models. The goodness-of-fit measures for the component and item models were less convincing than those for the total scores.

To sum up the investigations reported in this chapter, it is clear that risk scores produced by both instruments are significantly associated with reconviction, so that the assessments they provide are meaningful as risk assessments. The analyses at component level indicate that on the whole the choice of components is contributing usefully to the effectiveness of the instruments. Overall, the results of the reconviction follow-up resemble those contained in the interim report on a smaller sample (Raynor et al. 1999). Both OGRS and LSI-R consistently predict reconviction slightly more accurately than ACE: the main reason for this is likely to be the absence of static criminal history factors in ACE, and the shorter history of development, testing and refinement. (Some possibilities for the further development of ACE are reviewed below in chapter 7.) It is interesting that factors that have proved to be predictive of reconviction in Canada appear also to be valid for England and Wales. When applied to women offenders only, all three instruments perform in a fashion which is roughly similar to their performance when they are applied to the sample as a whole. Also, all of them show a significant association with serious reconviction, but the association does not appear strong enough to justify reliance on any of them as a sole predictor of serious reconviction.

5   Reliability and disclosure effects

Reliability of the instruments when used by different officers

In evaluating the feasibility of any assessment instrument for use by probation staff, it is important to investigate inter-rater reliability, or the extent to which differences in assessment scores may reflect differences in assessors rather than in those being assessed. In the case of LSI-R, we were able to do this by drawing on two area-based experiments involving blind double assessment. In Gloucestershire, 25 probationers were assessed at the mid-point of their probation orders by two officers who interviewed them separately, without access to each others' scores or to any other LSI-R assessment in the file. A total of 16 Gloucestershire officers were involved in various combinations (for a full account of how the experiment was set up and conducted see Chambers and Anderson, 1999). In West Glamorgan, ten pre-sentence assessments were carried out by pairs of officers interviewing together, who then completed separate Quikscore forms without consulting each other. Six officers were involved.

The results in the two areas were slightly different. In Gloucestershire 20 pairs of assessment scores, or 80 per cent, fell within three points of each other, and the items most likely to show disagreement (i.e. more than five disagreements out of 25 trials) concerned involvement in organised activities, relationship with parents, mental health, and educational qualifications. In West Glamorgan, where the interviews were shared and the officers may have been more experienced with LSI-R, nine of the ten pairs fell within three points, and the only item with more than two disagreements concerned past mental health treatment (for example, did 'seeing a psychiatrist' count as treatment?). If both trials are added together, we have 35 pairs of which 29, or 83 per cent, fell within three points. The largest discrepancy, in Gloucestershire, was seven points.

It has not been feasible to undertake any comparable paired trials for ACE, but an analysis has been undertaken of assessments made by ten Warwickshire officers, who had each written at least 18 first assessments, to determine how far the particular officer emerged as a significant factor in predicting the ORS score. Again OGRS2 is used to control for variations in the assessed population. Table 5.1 summarises the results: only one officer appeared to have a significant impact on scoring levels independently of other factors. Two others appear somewhat divergent from the group but not to a statistically significant degree.

Table 5.1: **Consistency of ACE assessments by ten officers**

N=206

Officer	No. of 1st assts	OGRS2 score mean	SD	ACE ORS score Mean	SD	Ratio of OGRS/ACE	Signif. of PO (t)
1	21	53.2	23.8	11.5	6.4	4.62	.000
2	21	50.9	28.1	20.6	13.4	2.47	.834
3	25	52.1	27.6	22.4	15.4	2.32	.298
4	18	45.7	27.5	17.6	10.4	2.59	.550
5	20	55.1	20.7	19.8	7.0	2.79	.584
6	23	65.0	28.3	20.4	11.7	3.20	.184
7	18	37.3	20.6	12.9	10.0	2.88	.064
8	19	48.1	25.6	23.2	12.7	2.07	.111
9	19	48.4	26.8	24.1	13.0	2.01	.054
10	22	49.6	29.4	18.7	13.8	2.65	.596
TOTAL	206	51.0	26.4	19.2	12.2	2.65	

Overall, the evidence on inter-rater reliability for LSI-R and ACE is not directly comparable owing to the different methods used; however, both instruments appear reasonably robust in this respect, at least in the current probation service context where few other consistent means of assessment are available. It would be advisable to carry out further studies on this issue as probation services become more used to the instruments: the quality of assessments may improve with practice, or it may deteriorate as the innovation effect is lost and management attention is diverted on to newer developments. In any case, continued monitoring of reliability would seem to be desirable in maintaining the integrity of the assessment process.

Disclosure effects

'Disclosure effects' can be said to occur when repeat assessments yield higher risk or needs scores because the offender has chosen to disclose more problems or the officer has learned more about the offender, rather than because risk or need factors have actually changed. This is a particular problem with instruments intended to measure progress under supervision, since an apparent deterioration may be due simply to disclosure effects (as suggested by Aubrey and Hough, 1997). Anecdotal evidence from practitioners suggested that disclosure effects might be particularly likely to cause differences between assessments made before sentence and assessments made after sentence, on commencement of supervision: for example, some officers suggested that illegal drug use was more likely to be disclosed after sentence. It was not possible to compare pre-sentence and commencement assessments on the same offenders, as people are usually subject to one or the other rather than both; however, Table 5.2 compares PSR-stage and commencement–stage scores on both instruments, again using OGRS2 scores (not vulnerable to disclosure effects) as a control. Scores on both instruments under the two conditions show small but significant differences, whereas OGRS2 scores do not.

Table 5.2: *Disclosure effects: overall ACE and LSI scores*

Sample	Score type	PSR stage Mean score	Commencement stage Mean score	Commencement /PSR Ratio*
LSI-R N=948	LSI-R	19.61	23.40	1.19 *
	OGRS2	50.36	47.37	0.94
		N=809	N=139	
ACE N=826	ACE	20.51	24.08	1.17 *
	OGRS2	48.82	51.72	1.06
		N=729	N=97	

* Indicates a significant t-test of the difference of the means (p<.01)
Source: LSI-R and ACE data; Home Office OGRS2 calculations

Table 5.3 shows which risk factors appear to be contributing to this difference. Most factors show no disclosure effect. Among those that do change, drugs emerge as important, together with other items which may be calling for a more subjective judgement from the officer. Further evidence is provided by one of the LSI-R-using areas which changed during the course of the study from undertaking commencement stage assessment to PSR-stage assessment (see table 5.4). Differences in the total scores may be partly to do with differences between the PSR population and those who are sentenced to some form of supervision (for example, the latter may have more problems), but what is interesting is that for some items the difference is proportionately rather greater than for the overall scores. Again these include items related to substance abuse, and emotional/personal items. (Among the ACE items, 'other habits' refers to substance abuse other than alcohol or drugs, such as solvent abuse. In any case 'other habit', 'learning ability' and 'discriminatory attitudes' have such small values that they may not be useful tests of disclosure effects.)

Table 5.3: Disclosure effects: selected factors which illustrate effects in PSR and commencement stages

Item/component	Pre-sentence report Mean	Commencement Mean	Commencement/ PSR Ratio
LSI-R			
Unemployment	0.68	0.84	1.23 *
Alcohol/ drugs	1.34	2.03	1.51 *
Alcohol only	0.72	1.05	1.46 *
Drugs only	0.62	0.97	1.58 *
Emotional/ personal	0.75	1.50	1.99 *
N=805	N=658	N=147	
ACE			
Drugs	0.65	1.11	1.70 *
Thinks reoffending inevitable	0.54	0.89	1.48 *
Other habit	0.04	0.20	5.00 *
Learning ability	0.09	0.26	2.90 *
Interpersonal skills	0.33	0.58	1.75 *
Welcomes supervision	0.58	0.84	1.45 *
Discriminatory attitudes	0.09	0.23	2.56 *
N=826	N=729	N=97	

* Indicates a significant t-test of the difference of the means (p<.01 after adjustment)
Source: LSI-R and ACE data (excluding ACE cases where first assessment was at release stage).

Table 5.4: Disclosure effects in one area (LSI-R only)

	PSR stage (from April 1998) Mean score	Commencement stage (before April 1998) Mean score	Commencement /PSR Ratio
LSI-R	18.53	23.54	1.27 *
Leisure	0.93	1.32	1.42 *
Alcohol/drugs	1.32	2.05	1.56 *
Alcohol only	0.68	1.07	1.58 *
Drugs only	0.64	0.99	1.54 *
Emotional/personal	0.68	1.51	2.21 *
N=307	N=161	N=146	

* Indicates a significant t-test of the difference of the means (p<.01 after adjustment)
Source: LSI-R data: PSR stage on or after 1.1.98; commencement stage before 1.1.98

Although the findings on disclosure effects are a little unclear, the most likely interpretation appears to be that both LSI-R and ACE show small disclosure effects related to stage of assessment, particularly concerning issues where the offender is likely to disclose more after sentence (for example, drug use) and perhaps some issues where the officer may be finding out more about personal and emotional difficulties. However, the effects are not large, and the next chapter explores the use of the instruments as change measures despite the small disclosure effects which may be present.

Risk-related change measurement

A dynamic risk/needs instrument should be capable of providing a risk-related measure of change. In other words, unlike a static predictor it should be able to register changes in criminogenic needs over time (whether or not these result from beneficial effects of supervision) which are reflected in real changes in the risk of reconviction. A number of offenders in both ACE and LSI-R samples had been reassessed during the course of supervision. Table 6.1 shows the reconviction rates for all those whose reassessment scores were different from their initial scores. This is done separately for those who started as high scorers and those who started as low scorers, to reduce the possibility that differences in reconviction simply reflect initial scores.

Table 6.1: **Changes in ACE and LSI-R scores between first and second assessments and reconviction (excluding no change in total score)**

Changes in ACE scores

First assessment	Direction of change in score	First assessment Mean	sd	% reconvicted	Significance (x^2)
'Low' N=85	Increasing N=22	12.55	5.39	68.2%	.000
	Decreasing N=63	14.87	4.59	20.6%	
'High' N=82	Increasing N=29	31.03	8.35	69.0%	.011
	Decreasing N=53	31.75	8.56	39.6%	
Total N=167		22.73	11.02	41.3%	

Changes in LSI-R scores

First assessment	Direction of change in score	First assessment Mean	sd	% reconvicted	Significance (x^2)
'Low' N=73	Increasing N=31	15.16	4.49	54.8%	.013
	Decreasing N=42	13.55	4.44	26.2%	
'High' N=84	Increasing N=37	27.6	3.82	78.4%	.027
	Decreasing N=47	27.72	5.62	55.3%	
Total N=157		21.42	8.20	52.8%	

It is clear that for both instruments, increasing scores are significantly associated with higher reconvictions and decreasing scores with lower reconvictions. It also appears that the association is stronger in the ACE cases. Table 6.2 shows which components changed in those cases which showed change, and in what proportion of cases each component changed. This information is more useful in the ACE cases, since a larger number of those had full component information available; a number of LSI-R cases which would have been relevant for this analysis were excluded when it was decided that reconviction searches could be undertaken only on a sample of cases rather than on all. In the ACE cases, all components except motivation showed overall improvement, including those identified by the regression analysis as particularly related to reconviction, such as substance abuse, lifestyle and pro-criminal attitudes.

Table 6.2: Proportion of cases in which scores change between first and second assessments.

ACE

ACE COMPONENTS

(N=173, reconviction rate 41%)	% of cases in which score increases	% of cases in which score decreases	% of cases showing any change	Significance of mean change
Accommodation	9	21	30	.007
Employment	13	30	43	.004*
Finances	10	31	41	.007
Family/personal relations	13	30	43	.001*
Substance abuse	11	34	45	.000***
Health	10	28	38	.001*
Personal skills	12	38	50	.000***
Individual characteristics	20	54	74	.000***
Lifestyle & associates	17	43	60	.000***
Attitudes	26	49	75	.000***
Motivation	41	31	72	.015
Total offender-related score	30	67	97	.000***

LSI-R

LSI-R COMPONENTS

(N=43, reconviction rate 76%)	% of cases in which score increases	% of cases in which score decreases	% of cases showing any change	Significance of mean change
Criminal history	63	-	63	.000**
Education/employment	42	19	61	.016
Financial	19	16	35	.341
Family/marital	28	30	58	.579
Accommodation	33	14	47	.070
Leisure/recreation	28	9	37	.006
Companions	35	12	47	.034
Alcohol/drug problem	33	26	59	.046
Emotional/personal	14	14	28	.268
Attitudes/orientation	31	26	57	1.000
Total LSI-R score	70	21	91	.000***

(The asterisks denote the usual three significance levels corrected for multiple t-tests)

Another way to look at these differences is to examine differences in scoring between reconvicted and unreconvicted cases, rather than differences in reconviction between score increasers and score decreasers. Figure 6.1 shows the movement in scores for reconvicted and unreconvicted offenders assessed on each instrument. The same relationship between score changes and reconviction is illustrated as appears in Table 6.1, and it is also apparent that those who avoided reconviction show, on average, larger downward changes in scores than the upward changes shown by those who reconvicted. Again the ACE scores show larger changes, which may be due to the fact that ACE consists only of change-sensitive dynamic items: a characteristic which probably reduces its effectiveness as a predictor may be more appropriate in its original role as an instrument for evaluating supervision by measuring change. Overall, however, it is clear that both instruments are capable of making a useful contribution as risk-related change measures. Both appear sensitive to change, and the changes they measure are related to risk of reconviction. It is also interesting that probation officers' judgements about what has changed prove significantly related to the 'harder' measure of reconviction: our findings suggest that practitioners' judgement, often criticised as unreliable, is in fact a good indicator when it forms part of the application of a structured instrument.

Figure 6.1: *Score changes and reconviction*

ACE ORS score change and reconviction (N=173)

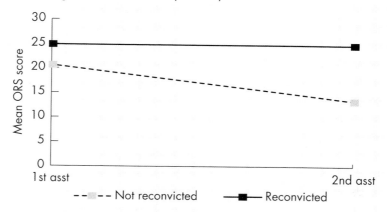

LSI-R score change and reconviction (N=187)

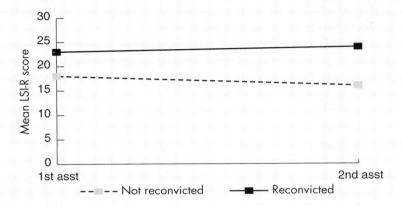

7   Further developments in the instruments

The LSI-R Screening Version (LSI-R-SV) and other LSI developments

During the course of the research we were informed that a 'screening version' of the LSI-R had been developed in Canada (Andrews and Bonta, 1998) based on a limited number of items believed to discriminate particularly well between people with low and high risks of reconviction, and it has now been made available as a scale containing just eight items from the full LSI-R (items 2, 5, 11, 24, 34, 43, 50 and 51 of the Quikscore version, though presented in a different order). Clearly these do not constitute a full needs assessment (such as would be needed, for example, to prepare a supervision plan), but the LSI-R Screening Version is intended to provide a quick and reasonably reliable method of screening offender populations to decide in which cases a full risk/needs assessment would be indicated.

Screening version scores are grouped into three bands, minimum, medium and maximum, with full assessment 'strongly recommended' for the medium band and 'mandatory' for the maximum band. It is possible to simulate application of the LSI-R-SV in our sample by selecting the relevant items. Table 7.1 summarises the distribution of the LSI-R sample in the LSI-R-SV risk bands, with the reconviction rate for each band, and Table 7.2 compares the percentages of reconvictions correctly predicted by LSI-R-SV and OGRS2. The screening version items also form one of the models explored by logistic regression in Table B.4 of Appendix B. It is clear that the screening version is predicting about as well as the full version, and further investigation of the screening version would probably be useful.

Table 7.1:   LSI-R-SV: levels of risk and reconviction

LSI-R-SV group		Not reconvicted		Reconvicted		More serious reconviction		Custodial reconviction	
	N	N	%	N	%	N	%	N	%
Minimum (0,1,2)	278	216	78	62	22	8	3	8	3
Medium (3,4,5)	411	220	54	191	46	18	5	31	8
Maximum (6,7,8)	116	43	37	73	63	16	15	22	19
Total	805	479	60	326	40	42	6	61	8

Table 7.2   Differences in LSI-R-SV and OGRS2 between cases which are reconvicted and not reconvicted over a 12-month period

Score type	Value range predicting non-reconviction	Value range predicting reconviction	% correctly predicted***	% false negative
N= 751				
LSI-R-SV	0-3	4-8	65.2***	16.5
OGRS2	≤56	>56	68.4***	15.5

*** χ^2 level of significance <.001

Other LSI-R related developments have been taking place during this study: for example, a version for young offenders has been under development for some time and, at the 1999 American Society of Criminology conference in Toronto, the Ontario Correctional Services demonstrated an enhanced online risk/need assessment and case management instrument called the Level of Service Inventory: Ontario Revision (LSI-OR). This is used in all Ontario correctional services, whether custodial or community-based, and assessments are carried out on the computer, integrated into the case record and accessible by all authorised personnel through their workstations. This system-wide adoption of a common assessment and planning instrument resembles what is intended for OASys in England and Wales. However, such developments lie outside the scope of this research.

Developments in ACE

The information collected for this study has made it possible to explore a number of possible developments in ACE, mainly directed towards improving the accuracy of risk prediction by changing the range of items included or adding static factors to the scoring.

Addition of static factors

The first stage was to include some 'static' factors which have been found predictive in previous studies. Some of these are genuinely unchanging, for example, sex, while others could better be described as 'status' variables for example, age, number of previous convictions, currently unemployed. They are listed in table 7.3. The first six are routinely collected ACE items. The criminal history items were supplied by the Home Office from PNC data since they were not routinely collected by services. These factors were tested for their significance in predicting reconviction within 12 months. All were significant at the .05 level or better (χ^2). They were all treated as binary variables and scored three (high risk) or zero (low risk) to match the range of the offending-related scores.

Table 7.3: Static factors tested

	High risk (score=3)	Low risk (score=0)
1. Sex	Male	Female
2. Age	under 23	23 plus
3. Accommodation status	other temporary/NFA	all other values
4. Employment status	registered unemployed	Ditto
5. Financial status	on state benefits/no income	Ditto
6. Family status	living with other family/other adults	Ditto
7. Total previous convictions	3+	0 - 2
8. Previous convictions in last 2 years	2+	0 - 1
9. Total previous custody	1+	None
10. Total previous youth custody	1+	None

Factor analysis

The total number of items for testing was 33 dynamic items (from ORS) and ten 'static' items described above. From these, 29 were selected for testing on the basis of their:

- predictive validity (association with reconviction significant at .05 level or better)

- discriminatory ability (items with frequencies below 10% were excluded).

Appendix A gives the details of this selection. Factor analysis was used to check the underlying structure and validity of these items, and the results are shown in table 7.4.

Table 7.4:   Factor analysis of 29 tested items

N=964

Factor 1 (13% of variance, alpha=.84) Attitudes/motivation	Factor 2 (12% of variance, alpha=.82) Lifestyle/accommodation	Factor 3 (9% of variance, alpha=.81) Criminal history
Accept responsibility for offending Acknowledge harm to victim Concern for close people Motivated to deal w. problems Motivated not to reoffend Pro-criminal attitudes	Drugs Lifestyle offending risk Associates offending risk Thinks reoffending likely Temporary accomm/NFA Accommodation OR Employment OR Finances OR	Previous custody Previous youth custody 3+ previous convictions 2+ preconvictions in last 2 years
Factor 4 (8% of variance, alpha=.71) Personal/social skills	Factor 5 (7% of variance, alpha=.74) Unemployment/poverty	Factor 6 (5% of variance) Age
Reasoning Impulsiveness Responsibility/control	Unemployed Living on benefits	Aged under 23
Factor 7 (4% of variance) Family situation	Factor 8 (4% of variance) Sex	
Living with other family/adults	Male	

The factor analysis produced eight factors with an eigenvalue >1, explaining altogether 62 per cent of the variance. This suggests that propensity to reoffend is multidimensional, and does not just consist of one major causation. Most items were strongly associated with one factor, but three items were dropped at this stage because they did not have such an association (loading <.5). These were interpersonal skills, boredom and having anti-criminal associates. Employment and finances offending-related problems fitted best into Group 2, but were also on the borderline of Group 5. Factors 1, 2 and 4 are still largely composed of dynamic items. There is again a clear 'Lifestyle' group including drugs, a 'Motivation' group and a 'Personal/social skills' group. However, the other five factors are made up of the new 'static' items, and there is surprisingly little overlap between the two. Criminal history forms a clear group. The data suggests that employment and finance could be thought of as a single component. There is also some evidence for considering personal skills and individual characteristics as a single 'Personal/Social skills' component. The internal reliability of each factor grouping was checked by ensuring that the items were highly correlated with each other. Cronbach's alpha was above .5 in all cases.

Logistic regression

The remaining 26 items were tested in combination as predictors of reconviction using logistic regression. The aim was to improve on the predictive validity of ORS. A summary of the results is given in Table 7.5 below. First the static items were tested on their own. These were entered using the Forward LR method, which allows the model to select predictor variables until overall accuracy cannot be further improved. Only four predictors were selected by the model: previous convictions in the last two years, employment status, age and previous custody. These four items correctly predicted reconviction in 68.1 per cent of cases with 17.3 per cent false negatives. This is more accurate than OGRS2 in Table 4.7, but the comparison should be viewed with caution, as results will always be better using the construction sample rather than an independent validation sample.

Model one: 26 item predictor

The first model tested all 26 dynamic and static items. These were all entered at once using the Entry method, and the resulting model was 70.6 per cent accurate with 14.1 per cent false negatives. A new 26 item predictor was constructed by adding together the item scores as when calculating the Offending-Related Score. As can be seen from Table 7.5, this scale was only 65.0 per cent accurate, a sharp reduction from when the items are entered individually. This is because the simple addition of item scores, although straightforward to calculate, is less sophisticated than the way logistic regression combines the items.

Model two: seven-item predictor

The second model tested the same 26 items, but using the Forward LR method. This time seven items were selected as shown in Table 7.5. The model was 70.5 per cent accurate with 14.5 per cent false negatives. Four of the items are 'static' and three are 'dynamic', indicating that both types have a role to play in prediction. The factors disclosed by the factor analysis are unevenly represented: two items come from factor 2 (lifestyle), two from factor 3 (criminal history), one each from factors 3, 4 and 5, but none from factor 1 (attitudes/motivation). A seven-item predictor was constructed as for model one. (This resembles in some respects the LSI-R Screening Version.) The predictor achieves a respectable accuracy level of 68.6 per cent, making it comparable to OGRS and LSI-R. Having seven items, this 'short' predictor has a score range from 0 to 21. The mean score is 7.0 and standard deviation 4.8. Figure 7.1 shows its ability to predict reconviction across the score range. Compared to ORS it has an improved spread of reconviction rates from 16 per cent (bottom quintile) to 76 per cent (top quintile).

Figure 7.1   'Short' ACE-based predictor scores and reconviction

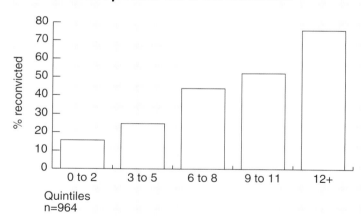

Model three: 10-item predictor

The third model was based on the seven items from model two, but adding in three items to achieve fuller coverage of the factors identified by the factor analysis. These additional items were family situation (factor 7), pro-criminal attitudes (factor 1) and lifestyle offending risk (factor 2). Although these items fall below statistical significance when added to the logistic regression, they should give the scale greater robustness if the factors are indicative. This model was also 70.5 per cent accurate. A 10-item predictor was constructed as previously, and the accuracy was 68.6 per cent - the same as the short seven-item version (see Table 7.5). Being a 10-item scale the score range is 0-30 with a mean of 9.4 and standard deviation of 6.0. The spread of reconviction rates is very similar to those in figure 7.1 above, ranging from 15 per cent (bottom quintile) to 74 per cent (top quintile).

Summary of potential developments in ACE

This chapter has shown that it is possible to add static factors to improve the predictive accuracy of ACE. The factor analysis shows that criminal history is a clear, separate factor, as are age and sex. The regression analysis shows that a combination of static and dynamic items can provide a satisfactory prediction of reconviction over 12 months. Three possible predictors were constructed, which give accuracy levels between 65 per cent and 69 per cent in this sample, the shorter ones being more accurate but the longer ones giving fuller coverage of components which are all individually associated with reconviction. This is summarised in Table 7.5. All would require validation through testing on other samples of offenders.

Table 7.5:   Summary of alternative ACE predictors

Revised component	Item	Static or dynamic	26-item model	10-item model	7-item model
1. Personal	1. Male	S	✓		
	2. Age under 23	S	✓	✓	✓
2. Criminal history	3. More than 2 preconvictions	S	✓	✓	
	4. More than 1 in last 2 years	S	✓	✓	✓
	5. Any previous custody	S	✓	✓	✓
	6. Any previous youth custody	S	✓		
3. Accomm. and neighbourhood	7. Other temp accomm. or NFA	S	✓		
	8. Accommodation OR	D	✓		
4. Employment and finances	9. Registered unemployed	S	✓	✓	✓
	10. ETE OR	D	✓		
	11. On state benefits/no income	S	✓		
	12. Finances OR	D	✓		
5. Family and personal relationships	13. Living with other family/ adults	S	✓	✓	
6. Substance abuse	14. Drugs OR	D	✓	✓	✓
7. Personal and social skills	15. Reasoning/thinking skills OR	D	✓		
	16. Impulsiveness/risk taking OR	D	✓	✓	✓
	17. Responsibility/control OR	D	✓		
8. Lifestyle and associates	18. Lifestyle causes offending risk	D	✓	✓	
	19. Friends/associates cause risk	D	✓		
9. Attitudes and motivation	20. Accepts responsibility for offending	D	✓		
	21. Acknowledges harm to victim	D	✓		
	22. Concern about effects on 'close' people	D	✓		
	23. Has pro-criminal attitudes	D	✓	✓	
	24. Regards further offending as inevitable	D	✓	✓	✓
	25. Motivated to avoid re-offending	D	✓		
	26. Motivated to deal with relevant problems	D	✓		
TOTAL SCORE			0-78	0-30	0-21
% correctly predicted			65.0%	68.6%	68.6%
Pseudo R^2			.199	.246	.239

8   Conclusion: the feasibility and prospects of risk/need assessment in the probation service

This chapter summarises the key findings from the study, and considers their implications for the future of risk/need assessment in UK probation services. Firstly, the study shows that risk/need instruments can be used effectively in UK probation services: they produce information about needs, and they can provide estimates of the risk of reconviction. The LSI-R, which includes some 'static' risk factors and has a longer history of development, provides a slightly more accurate risk assessment than ACE, and approaches the effectiveness of the established and sophisticated 'static' predictor OGRS. However, all three instruments need to be supplemented by other forms of assessment before they provide a reliable guide to the likelihood of serious reoffending. Their main contribution in this area would probably be to provide threshold scores and trigger items pointing to the need for further assessment.

Both instruments show some 'disclosure effects' which lead to higher scores if offenders are assessed after sentencing rather than before. This appears partly attributable to offenders' greater willingness to disclose drug use after sentence, but other factors, including emotional and personal functioning, also tend to show disclosure effects. However, these appear to be small and have only a marginal effect on the use of the instruments for risk assessment or change measurement.

Both LSI-R and ACE can be reliably used over limited time periods (usually six months in this study) as measures of risk-related change. This is something which a solely static predictor such as OGRS2 cannot provide. ACE was slightly more effective in measuring such changes than LSI-R, probably because it contains a larger number of solely dynamic items. It has become essential that policy-makers and those delivering and implementing various penal sanctions (Prison and Probation Services) have available reliable means of measuring the relative impact of different penal sanctions and particular types or modes of intervention, on the subsequent offending behaviour of offenders subject to them. The current Home Office Pathfinder Programme and the accreditation of programmes both require evidence of the effectiveness of the programmes being developed and implemented. This will require structured means of assessment and re-assessment which can be reliably used to measure changes in offenders, which in turn are known to be indicative of changes in reoffending and reconvictions. The findings in this study about the benefits of having dynamic factors in LSI-R and particularly in ACE indicate the potential for the use of such factors individually and in combination as change measures. Such changes can be identified well in advance of changes in reconviction levels, and can provide some information about which particular factors are being affected by which particular types or modes of intervention.

Both LSI-R and ACE appear reasonably reliable when used by different assessors. In the case of LSI-R it has been possible to test this directly in dual assessments, whilst for ACE it has been investigated by measuring how far differences in the administering officer account for variation in scores. The overall results of this study show the importance of dynamic factors as predictors and particularly as measures of change. These dynamic factors require assessors to make careful judgements of the evidence or importance of different items in both instruments. Those judgements are usually distilled from secondary information in records and reports, information provided directly in interview with offenders and others, and observations of behaviour and non-verbal communication. The investigation in this study into the use of the instruments by different assessors indicates that all but a small minority of the probation officers who completed the assessments and re-assessments not only did them consistently, but also demonstrated reasonably reliable judgements in respect of dynamic factors. Both instruments appear robust enough for general probation use, but this does not rule out the possibility that standards of use could slip, and continuing attention to quality control and maintenance is likely to be useful. It is also possible to develop these instruments further: for example, a shortened version of LSI-R is shown to be a good predictor, as are several possible modified versions of ACE. Improving prediction by selecting out particularly predictive items can, however, be at the cost of reducing comprehensiveness in the assessment of need.

Finally, the best features of both instruments are the outcome of a process of development and modification spanning six years in the case of ACE, and about 20 in the case of LSI-R. This has been particularly important in developing sufficient ease of use to allow them to become routine parts of practice. However well an instrument is capable of performing in principle, it will only perform well in practice if it can be developed and offered in a form which probation officers and others can actually use and experience as at least reasonably helpful. This has implications for the development of new instruments: there is no point in achieving accuracy by making an instrument so comprehensive that it cannot be conveniently used.

Overall, this research documents the relatively successful introduction of elements of risk/needs assessment into UK probation services, and suggests that they can make a serious contribution to the development and evaluation of more effective practice. Their impact has been substantial during the short period during which they have been in use, and it is to be hoped that this trajectory of development can be maintained.

Table A.1: Summary of ACE components and scoring

Component	Item	Max Weight	Static/Dynamic
1. Accommodation and neighbourhood	1. Ditto	3	D
2. Employment, training and education	2. Ditto	3	D
3. Finances	3. Ditto	3	D
4. Family and personal relationships	4. Ditto	3	D
5. Substance abuse and addictions	5. Alcohol	3	D
	6. Drugs	3	D
	7. Gambling	3	D
	8. Other habit	3	D
6. Health	9. Physical health	3	D
	10. Mental health/Emotional well-being	3	D
7. Personal skills	11. Learning abilities/literacy	3	D
	12. Interpersonal/social skills	3	D
	13. Reasoning/thinking skills	3	D
8. Individual characteristics	14. Aggression/temper	3	D
	15. Boredom/need for excitement	3	D
	16. Impulsiveness/risk-taking	3	D
	17. Self esteem/self image	3	D
	18. Sexuality/sexual behaviour	3	D
	19. Discriminatory attitudes/behaviour	3	D
	20. Responsibility/control	3	D
	21. Other problem	3	D
9. Lifestyle and associates	22. Lifestyle causes risk of reoffending	3	D
	23. Friends/associates cause risk of reoffending	3	D
	24. Has anti-criminal friends/associates	3	D
10. Attitudes	25. Accepts responsibility for offending	3	D
	26. Acknowledges harm to victim	3	D
	27. Concerned about effects on 'close' people	3	D
	28. Has pro-criminal attitudes	3	D
	29. Regards further offending as inevitable	3	D
	30. Thinks benefits of crime outweigh costs	3	D
11. Motivation/attitude to supervision	31. Motivated to avoid reoffending	3	D
	32. Motivated to deal with relevant problems	3	D
	33. Welcomes being under supervision	3	D
TOTAL SCORE		99	

Table A.2: Summary of LSI-R components and scoring

Component	Items		Weight if all items score	Static/ dynamic
Criminal history	1-3	Prior convictions *	3	S
	4	Current charges	1	S
	5	Arrest under age 16 *	1	S
	6-10	Custody and institutional misconduct	5	S
Education/employment	11	Currently unemployed *	1	D
	12-14	Employment problems	3	S/D
	15-17	Schooling	3	S/D
	18-20	Poor rewards: performance, peers, authority	3	D
Financial	21-22	Problems & low fixed income	2	D
Family/marital	23	Current marital dissatisfaction	1	D
	24-25	Non-rewarding relatives *	2	D
	26	Convicted close relative	1	S/D
Accommodation	27-28	Dissatisfaction	2	D
	29	High crime neighbourhood	1	D
Leisure/recreation	30-31	Poor participation and use of time	2	D
Companions	32	Social isolation	1	D
	33-36	Attitude to crime of acquaintances/friends *	4	D
Alcohol/drug problem	37-38	Past alcohol or drugs problems	2	S
	39-40	Current alcohol or drugs problems	2	D
	41-45	Situational problems *	5	D
Emotional/personal	46-47	Abilities affected	2	D
	48-49	Past mental health treatment	2	S
	50	Psychological assessment indicator *	1	D
Attitudes/orientation	51-54	Supportive of crime and poor to sentence*	4	D
TOTAL	54		54	

* indicates inclusion of one item in Screening Version.

Table A.3: **Percentage of first assessment cases who had a risk/needs item and association of risk/needs item with reconviction (i.e. item level detail of component analysis in Tables 4.2, 4.3 and 4.11)**

a: ACE items N=1,186

Component	Item	% with risk	Sig. of association	
Accommodation and neighbourhood	Accommodation and neighbourhood	16	.000	***
Employment, training and education	Employment, training and education	28	.000	***
Finances	Finances	32	.000	***
Family/personal relationships	Family/personal relationships	26	.156	
Substance abuse and addictions	Alcohol	34	.052	
	Drugs	24	.000	***
	Gambling	2	.690	
	Other habit	2	.004	*
Health	Physical health	4	.221	
Personal skills	Mental health/emotional well-being	21	.480	
	Learning abilities/literacy	3	.045	
	Interpersonal/social skills	11	.001	*
	Reasoning/thinking skills	34	.012	
Individual characteristics	Aggression/temper	26	.208	
	Boredom/need for excitement	14	.000	***
	Impulsiveness/risk-taking	35	.000	***
	Self esteem/self image	17	.178	
	Sexuality/sexual behaviour	2	.564	
	Discriminatory attitudes/behaviour	4	.658	
	Responsibility/control	30	.000	***
	Other problem	2	.731	
Lifestyle and associates	Lifestyle causes risk of reoffending	39	.000	***
	Friends/associates cause risk of reoffending	33	.000	***
	Has anti-criminal friends/associates	36	.002	*
Attitudes	Accepts responsibility for offending	21	.010	
	Acknowledges harm to victim	38	.002	*
	Concerned about effects on 'close' people	25	.000	***
	Has pro-criminal attitudes	19	.000	***
	Regards further offending as inevitable	13	.000	***
	Thinks benefits of crime outweigh costs	8	.000	***
Motivation	Motivated to avoid reoffending	11	.000	***
	Motivated to deal with relevant problems	17	.000	***
	Welcomes being under supervision	20	.937	

b: LSI-R items N=805

Component	Items	% with risk	Sig. of association	
Criminal history	Prior convictions: any adult	81	.000	***
	Prior convictions: 2 +	69	.000	***
	Prior convictions: 3 +	59	.000	***
	Current charges: 3 +	34	.094	
	Arrest under age 16	40	.000	***
	Custodial sentence	38	.000	***
	Escape from custodial/residential institution	2	.023	
	Punishment for institutional misconduct	9	.014	
	Charged during community supervision	30	.000	***
	Record of assault/violence	43	.001	*
	Currently unemployed	71	.000	***
Education/ employment	Frequent unemployment	57	.000	***
	No continuous employment	38	.000	***
	Dismissed	24	.292	
	School: minimal	70	.000	*
	School: no qualifications	58	.001	*
	School: exclusions	28	.000	***
	Poor rewards: performance	74	.000	***
	Poor rewards: peers	74	.000	***
	Poor rewards: authority	74	.000	***
Financial	Problems	53	.000	***
	Low fixed income	71	.000	***
Family/marital	Current marital dissatisfaction	34	.146	
	Poor rewards: parents	34	.000	*
	Poor rewards: other relatives	27	.012	
	Convicted close relative	27	.022	
Accommodation	Dissatisfaction	22	.000	**
	Frequent moves	23	.000	**
	High crime neighbourhood	35	.000	***
Leisure/recreation	Poor participation	65	.000	**
	Poor use of time	53	.000	***
Companions	Social isolation	15	.371	
	Criminal acquaintances	73	.000	***
	Criminal friends	59	.000	***
	No anti-criminal acquaintances	19	.000	**
	No anti-criminal friends	22	.000	**

Component	Items	% with risk	Sig. of association	
Alcohol/drug problem	Past alcohol problem	49	.034	
	Past drug problem	42	.000	***
	Current alcohol problem	30	.159	
	Current drug problem	26	.000	***
	Situational problem: law	50	.011	
	Situational problem: marital	35	.000	**
	Situational problem: school/work	20	.000	*
	Situational problem: medical	19	.000	**
	Situational problem: other	9	.037	
Emotional/ personal	Abilities affected	38	.267	
	Abilities severely affected	4	.943	
	Past mental health treatment	21	.291	
	Present mental health treatment	10	.115	
	Psychological assessment indicator	15	.991	
Attitudes/ orientation	Supportive of crime	30	.001	*
	Unconventional	23	.000	**
	Poor to sentence	15	.007	
	Poor to supervision	13	.007	

(1) Independent samples t-test. Significance levels (after adjustment for multiple t-tests):   *=<.05   **=<.01
   ***=<.001

Table A4 Static and dynamic factors tested for revised ACE predictor (see chapter 7)

All items are scored in the range 0-3. Static factors score 0 or 3.

'OR' is short for 'is offending related' (frequency = % of maximum)   N=964

Component	Item	Frequency	Association with reconviction*	Test?
1. Personal	1. Male**	88%	.020	Yes
	2. Age under 23**	40%	.000	Yes
2. Criminal history	3. More than 2 preconvictions**	52%	.000	Yes
	4. More than 1 in last 2 years**	34%	.000	Yes
	5. Any previous custody**	35%	.000	Yes
	6. Any previous youth custody**	25%	.000	Yes
3. Accomm. and	7. Other temp accomm. or NFA**	15%	.000	Yes
neighbourhood	8. Accommodation OR	16%	.000	Yes
4. Employment,	9. Registered unemployed**	44%	.000	Yes
training and ed.	10. ETE OR	28%	.000	Yes
5. Finances	11. On state benefits/no income**	63%	.000	Yes
	12. Finances OR	32%	.000	Yes
6. Family and	13. Living with other family/other adults**	10%	.006	Yes
personal rels.	14. Relationships OR	26%	.156	No
7. Substance abuse	15. Alcohol OR	34%	.052	No
	16. Drugs OR	24%	.000	Yes
	17. Gambling OR	2%	.690	No
	18. Other habit OR	2%	.004	No
8. Health	19. Physical health OR	4%	.221	No
	20. Mental health OR	21%	.480	No
9. Personal skills	21. Learning abilities/literacy OR	3%	.045	No
	22. Interpersonal/social skills OR	11%	.001	Yes
	23. Reasoning/thinking skills OR	34%	.012	Yes
10. Individual	24. Aggression/temper OR	26%	.208	No
characteristics	25. Boredom/need for excitement OR	14%	.000	Yes
	26. Impulsiveness/risk taking OR	35%	.000	Yes
	27. Self esteem/self image OR	17%	.178	No
	28. Sexuality/sexual behaviour OR	2%	.564	No
	29. Discriminatory attitudes OR	4%	.658	No
	30. Responsibility/control OR	30%	.000	Yes
	31. Other problem OR	2%	.731	No
11. Lifestyle and	32. Lifestyle causes offending risk	39%	.000	Yes
associates	33. Friends/associates cause risk	33%	.000	Yes
	34. Has anti-criminal associates	36%	.002	Yes
12. Attitudes	35. Accepts responsibility for offending	21%	.010	Yes
	36. Acknowledges harm to victim	38%	.002	Yes
	37. Concern about effects on 'close' people	25%	.000	Yes
	38. Has pro-criminal attitudes	19%	.000	Yes
	39. Regards further offending as inevitable	13%	.000	Yes
	40. Thinks benefits of crime outweigh costs	8%	.000	No
13. Motivation	41. Motivated to avoid reoffending	11%	.000	Yes
	42. Motivated to deal with relevant problems	17%	.000	Yes
	43. Welcomes being under supervision	20%	.937	No

* t-test or χ^2 significance level ** 'static' item

Appendix B: Logistic regression

Multivariate analysis is required to isolate the importance of any one particular scale (ACE ORS, LSI-R, LSI-SV or OGRS), component or item of the scale in the risk of reconviction. Logistic regression was used because the dependent variable is binary (not reconvicted versus reconvicted during a 12-month follow-up period). The logistic regression models are based on data sets for which both OGRS and either ACE or LSI-R were available. The current state of development of ACE precludes validation of the ACE models. The LSI-R models are validated (using construction and hold-out samples), and the results are similar to those from discriminant analysis (Andrews and Bonta, 1996). There is evidence that interactions between the financial and employment components or items can occur, and this would explain the selection of one or other component in different countries or populations.

For simplicity, only main effects models are presented here (that is, models which assume that the effect of a given factor is the same for all groups of offenders). It is possible to test for interaction between risk factors to see if they operate differently for different sub-groups of offenders (such as women, those reconvicted of more serious offences or given a custodial sentence), but interaction models are often difficult to interpret for sub-groups which make up small proportions of samples. Area has been tested as an independent and external factor: in the LSI-R model, as one area's accommodation problems otherwise exerted some leverage over the models. (Outliers and cases with high leverage have been retained in the samples.)

Interpretation of the models

The results presented here include only those independent variables which are statistically related to reconviction. The scale total score, component and item scores were selected if the t-statistic (Table 4.5) showed significance ($p < .05$) after adjustment for multiple t-testing by a Bonferroni correction (SPSS 1998:105).

Statistics which indicate model calibration and discrimination are included only for the total score models in order to avoid over-interpretation of the component and item models, in which leverage and a poor fit for sub-groups could distort results. The component and item models should be interpreted as informative rather than explanatory.

- Coefficient B: the coefficient is the measure of the changes in the ratio of probabilities of reconviction to no reconviction expressed in logarithms, and is included to indicate the sign of the change. A positive coefficient indicates an increased risk of reconviction, and a negative coefficient indicates a decreased risk of reconviction, with a unit change in the variable.

- EXP(B): the exponential (or antilog) of the coefficient, known as the odds ratio, is easier to interpret than the coefficient. It is the odds of reconviction associated with one unit change in the variable for two offenders who are identical except in respect of this variable. If EXP(B) is greater than 1, this means that the odds of reconviction are increased, if EXP(B) is less than 1, the odds are decreased. For categorical variables, the effect of being in the category are compared to the effect of being in a reference category, and EXP(B) is interpreted as the odds of reconviction compared to the reference category (for which the odds ratio is 1).

- Significance: all coefficients are tested to see if they are statistically different to zero. * indicates the probability of this being less than 5 per cent, ** less than 1 per cent and *** less than 0.1 per cent.

- Goodness-of-fit: the model chi square tests the null hypothesis that the coefficients for all the variables in the model, except the constant, are zero. The null hypothesis is rejected if the probability of this is less than 5 per cent – in all the models the probability is less than .1 per cent.

- Model calibration: the Hosmer-Lemeshow goodness-of-fit chi square test indicates how closely the observed and predicted probabilities match. The values range from zero to one and higher values indicate a better fit (i.e. the chi square statistic is not significant).

- Model discrimination: the ability of the model to discriminate between the two groups (reconvicted and not reconvicted) is indicated by the c statistic, which measures the proportion of pairs of cases with different observed outcomes in which the model predicts a higher probability of reconviction for the reconvicted case than for the case which is not reconvicted. A value of 0.5 indicates that the model is no better than chance for assigning cases to groups, and a value of one indicates that the model always assigns higher probability to reconvicted cases.

On logistic regression using SPSS see SPSS (1999); for comparison with discriminant analysis see also Hair et al, (1998).

Table B.1:   *Single factor models of change in the risk of reconviction (12 months)*

Single factor model	Coefficient (B)	Odds ratio (Exp B)		95% confidence interval	
				Lower	Upper
ACE					
ACE ORS score (dynamic)	.0455	1.0466	***	1.0348	1.0584
Constant	-1.2466		***		
Model χ^2 69.455***					
Hosmer-Lemeshow .34					
C-statistic .66					
N=903					
OGRS on ACE data (static)	.0287	1.0291	***	1.0236	1.0347
Constant	-1.7536		***		
Model χ^2 124.108***					
Hosmer-Lemeshow .48					
C-statistic .71					
N=903					
LSI-R					
LSI-R (static/dynamic)	.0818	1.0852	***	1.0685	1.1022
Constant	-1.9956		***		
Model χ^2 123.617***					
Hosmer-Lemeshow .97					
C-statistic .71					
N=948					
OGRS on LSI-R data (static)	.0315	1.0320	***	1.0264	1.0375
Constant	-1.9319		***		
Model $\chi2$ 153.061***					
Hosmer-Lemeshow .13					
C-statistic .73					
N=948					

Table B.2: **Static and dynamic factor models of change in the risk of reconviction (12 months)**

Static and dynamic factor model	Coefficient (B)	Odds ratio (Exp B)		95% confidence interval	
				Lower	Upper
ACE ORS & OGRS					
ACE ORS	.0259	1.0263	***	1.0137	1.0390
OGRS2	.0241	1.0244	***	1.0185	1.0303
Constant	-2.0755		***		
Model χ^2 141.616***					
Hosmer-Lemeshow .16					
C-statistic .72					
N=903					
LSI-R (dynamic) & OGRS					
LSI-R (dynamic only)	.0643	1.0664	***	1.0407	1.0927
OGRS2	.0279	1.0283	***	1.0215	1.0352
Area 1	.2309	1.2598		.8223	1.9301
Area 2	-1.1674	.3112	*	.1250	.7749
Area 3	.5926	1.8087	**	1.2440	2.6298
Area 4	.0000	1.0000			
Constant	-2.7429		***		
Model χ^2 166.305***					
Hosmer-Lemeshow .44					
C-statistic .76					
N=742					

Table B.3: **Components which influence the risk of reconviction (12 months)**

Component model	Coefficient (B)	Odds ratio (Exp B)		95% confidence interval	
				Lower	Upper
ACE ORS components					
Substance abuse	.1599	1.1728	**	1.0752	1.2844
Lifestyle	.1361	1.1473	***	1.0681	1.2422
Attitudes	.0797	1.0828	**	1.0264	1.1329
Constant	-1.4443		***		
Model χ^2 95.546***					
N=881					
LSI-R components					
Financial	.4870	1.6274	***	1.3072	2.0260
Companions	.2992	1.3488	***	1.1800	1.5418
Criminal history	.1917	1.2113	***	1.1296	1.2990
Area 1	.1837	1.2017		.7981	1.8093
Area 2	-1.0018	.3672	*	.1543	.8736
Area 3	.5333	1.7046	**	1.1922	2.4372
Area 4 (reference)	.0000	1.0000			
Constant	-2.7087				
Model χ^2 132.029***					
N=749					

Table B.4:   Items which influence the risk of reconviction (12 months)

Item model	Coefficient (B)	Odds ratio (Exp B)		95% confidence interval	
				Lower	Upper
ACE ORS items					
Thinks reoffending inevitable	.4813	1.6181	***	1.3338	2.0711
Associates cause risk	.2544	1.2897	**	1.0773	1.5141
Drugs	.2087	1.2321	**	1.0695	1.4109
Impulsiveness	.1983	1.2194	**	1.0296	1.3627
Constant	-1.2245		***		
Model χ² 118.295***					
N=903					
LSI-R items					
Arrested under age 16	.4887	1.6302	*	1.0726	2.4777
No continuous employment	.5162	1.6757	*	1.0913	2.5731
Financial problems	.4654	1.5926	*	1.0542	2.4061
Low fixed income	.8502	2.3401	*	1.0665	5.1346
Criminal acquaintances	.8068	2.2408	*	1.1820	4.2479
Social isolation	-.5694	.5659	*	.3245	.9868
Supportive of crime	-.7436	.4754	*	.2647	.8536
Area 1	.1477	1.1592		.6917	1.9425
Area 2	-1.1020	.3322	*	.1162	.9498
Area 3	.6479	1.9115	**	1.2318	2.9664
Area 4 (reference)	.0000	1.0000			
Constant	-3.1997		***		
Model χ² 192.537***					
Hosmer-Lemeshow .71					
N=702					

LSI-R-SV					
Some criminal friends	1.0267	2.7919	***	1.9232	4.0529
Two or more prior convictions	.6451	1.9062	**	1.2962	2.8033
Currently unemployed	.6201	1.8591	**	1.2548	2.7544
Arrested under age 16	.5145	1.6729	**	1.1868	2.3580
Area 1	.1956	1.2161		.7799	1.8961
Area 2	-1.1785	.3077	*	.1183	.8006
Area 3	.6666	1.9476	**	1.3194	2.8748
Area 4 (reference)	.0000	1.0000			
Constant	-2.5918		***		

Model χ^2 127.726***

Hosmer-Lemeshow .72

N=751

References:

Hair, J. F., Anderson, R. E., Tatham, R. L. and Black, W. C. (1998) *Multivariate data analysis,* New Jersey: Prentice Hall, 5th edition.

SPSS (1998) *SPSS Base 8.0 Applications Guide,* Chicago: SPSS Inc.

SPSS (1999) *SPSS Regression Models 9.0,* Chicago: SPSS Inc.

Appendix C: LSI-R and ACE scores and
levels of reconviction

This appendix draws on our data to provide the nearest currently possible approximation to 'conversion tables' showing the average reconviction rate that can be expected from a group of offenders having a given LSI-R or ACE score. Several warnings are relevant. First, the samples are still not large compared to what would be desirable for this purpose, and larger samples would yield greater accuracy and confidence. Secondly, the reconviction figures are based on the PNC searches and are not therefore equivalent to the 'standard list' Offenders Index reconvictions generally used in OGRS-related reconviction studies. This may yield higher reconviction rates for high-scoring individuals: for example, at the higher-scoring end of the LSI-R table the reconviction rates exceed those estimated for individuals with similar LSI-R scores in Raynor 1998b, which included a table based on the relationship between LSI-R scores and OGRS scores. In both LSI-R and ACE tables the instrument scores are grouped into bands. These are broader for ACE than for LSI-R because the relationship between ACE ORS scores and reconviction is not considered close enough to support a finer calibration.

Table C.1: **LSI-R score groups and reconviction rates within 12 months**

| | All LSI-R cases (n=1,021) | |
Score group	% reconvicted	N
0-8	15	131
9-11	21	90
12-14	32	94
15-17	31	106
18-20	40	111
21-23	46	100
24-26	53	101
27-29	57	89
30-32	58	85
33-35	62	55
36+	86	59

Table C.2: ACE ORS score groups and reconviction rates within 12 months

Score group	ACE cases (n=903)	
	% reconvicted	N
0-8	22	146
9-15	34	183
16-26	46	295
27-39	53	181
40+	69	98

American Psychological Association (1985) *Standards for Educational and Psychological Testing.* Washington: American Psychological Association.

Andrews, D. A. (1982) *The Level of Supervision Inventory (LSI): the first follow-up.* Toronto: Ontario Ministry of Correctional Services.

Andrews, D.A. and Bonta, J. (1994) *The Psychology of Criminal Conduct.* Cincinnati: Anderson.

Andrews, D. A. and Bonta, J. (1995) *The Level of Service Inventory-Revised Manual.* Toronto: Multi-Health Systems Inc.

Andrews, D. A. and Bonta, J. (1998) *The Level of Service Inventory: Screening Version.* Toronto: Multi-Health Systems Inc.

Andrews, D. A., Zinger, I., Hoge, R. D., Bonta, J., Gendreau, P. and Cullen, F. T. (1990) 'Does correctional treatment work? A clinically relevant and psychologically informed meta-analysis'. *Criminology* 28, 369-404.

Aubrey, R. and Hough, M. (1997) *Assessing Offenders' Needs: assessment scales for the Probation Service.* Home Office Research Study No.166, London: Home Office.

Aye-Maung, N. and Hammond, N. (2000) *Risk of Reoffending and Needs Assessments: the User's Perspective.* Home Office Research Study No.216, London: Home Office, unpublished

Beck, U. (1992) *Risk Society: Towards a New Modernity.* London: Sage.

Bonta, J. (1993) *A Summary of Research Findings on the LSI.* Ottawa: unpublished.

Bonta, J. (1996) 'Risk-needs assessment and treatment' in A. Harland (ed.) *Choosing Correctional Options that Work.* London: Sage, 18-32.

Chambers, H. and Anderson, B. (1999) *Level of Service Inventory - Revised: research into inter-rater reliability.* Gloucester: Gloucestershire Probation Service, unpublished.

Clark, D. (1998) *Effective Regimes Measurement Research,* H. M. Prison Service: unpublished.

Copas, J. B. (1992) *Statistical analysis for a risk of reconviction predictor.* Report to the Home Office, University of Warwick: unpublished.

Davies, P. (1999) *Risk and Need Assessment in Devon Probation Service.* Dinas Powys: Cognitive Centre Foundation.

Feeley, M. and Simon, J. (1992) 'The new penology: notes on the emerging strategy of corrections and its implications'. *Criminology* 30, 449-474.

Feeley, M. and Simon, J. (1994) 'Actuarial justice: the emerging new criminal law' in D. Nelken (ed.) *The Futures of Criminology.* London: Sage.

Frude, N., Honess, T. and Maguire, M. (1994) *CRIME-PICS II Manual.* Cardiff: Michael and Associates.

Gendreau, P., Little, T. and Goggin, C. (1995) *A Meta-Analysis of the Predictors of Adult Offender Recidivism: Assessment Guidelines for Classification and Treatment.* Report to the Corrections Branch, Ministry Secretariat, Solicitor General of Canada, Saint John: University of New Brunswick.

Gibbs, A. (1999) 'The Assessment, Case Management and Evaluation System'. *Probation Journal* 46, 182-186.

Her Majesty's Inspectorate of Probation (HMIP) (1995) *Dealing with Dangerous People: the Probation Service and Public Protection.* London: Home Office.

Hollin, C. and Palmer, E. (1995) *Assessing Prison Regimes.* Report to HM Prison Service by the School of Psychology, University of Birmingham.

Home Office (1992) *National Standards for the Supervision of Offenders in the Community.* London: Home Office.

Home Office (1995) *National Standards for the Supervision of Offenders in the Community.* London: Home Office.

Home Office (1996) *Guidance for the Probation Service on the Offender Group Reconviction Scale.* Probation Circular 63/1996, London: Home Office.

Home Office (1999a) *Effective Practice Initiative: a joint risk/needs assessment system for the Prison and Probation Services.* Circular 16/1999, London: Home Office.

Home Office (1999b) *What Works: Reducing Reoffending: Evidence-Based Practice.* London: Home Office.

Home Office (1999c) *Programmes for offenders: guidance for evaluators.* Crime Reduction Programme Guidance Note 2, London: Home Office.

Kemshall, H. (1996) *Reviewing Risk: A review of research on the assessment of risk and dangerousness: implications for policy and practice in the Probation Service.* Birmingham: report to the Home Office Research and Statistics Directorate.

Lloyd, C., Mair, G. and Hough, M. (1994) *Explaining Reconviction Rates: a critical analysis.* Home Office Research Study No.136, London: HMSO.

May, C. (1999) *Explaining Reconviction Following a Community Sentence: the role of social factors.* Home Office Research Study No.192, London: Home Office.

McGuire, J., Broomfield, D., Robinson, C. and Rowson, B. (1995) 'Short-term impact of probation programs: an evaluative study'. *International Journal of Offender Therapy and Comparative Criminology* 39, 23-42.

OASys Project Team (1999) *The Offender Assessment System (OASys) Manual.* London: Home Office.

Raynor, P. (1997a) *Implementing the Level of Service Inventory - Revised in Britain: Report 1: Initial findings from the West Glamorgan Probation Service.* Dinas Powys: Centre for Criminal Justice and Criminology and Cognitive Centre Foundation.

Raynor, P. (1997b) *Implementing the Level of Service Inventory - Revised in Britain: Report 2: Initial results from five probation areas.* Dinas Powys: University of Wales, Swansea and Cognitive Centre Foundation.

Raynor, P. (1998a) 'Attitudes, Social Problems and Reconviction in the STOP probation experiment'. *Howard Journal* 37, 1-15.

Raynor, P. (1998b) *Implementing the Level of Service Inventory - Revised in Britain: Report 3: Risk and need assessment in the five pilot areas.* Dinas Powys: University of Wales, Swansea and Cognitive Centre Foundation.

Raynor, P., and Vanstone, M. (1994) *Straight Thinking On Probation: third interim evaluation report: reconvictions within 12 months.* Bridgend: Mid Glamorgan Probation Service.

Raynor, P. and Vanstone, M. (1996) 'Reasoning and Rehabilitation in Britain: the results of the Straight Thinking On Probation (STOP) programme'. *International Journal of Offender Therapy and Comparative Criminology* 40, 279-291.

Raynor, P. and Vanstone, M. (1997) *Straight Thinking On Probation (STOP): the Mid Glamorgan Experiment.* Probation Studies Unit Report 4, Oxford: Centre for Criminological Research.

Raynor, P., Kynch, J., Merrington, S. and Roberts, C. (1999) *Evaluating Risk and Need Assessment in Probation Services.* Interim Report to the Home Office, unpublished.

Roberts, C. and Robinson, G. (1998). 'Improving Practice Through Pilot Studies: the Case of Pre-Sentence Reports'. *VISTA* 3, 186-195.

Roberts, C., Burnett, R., Kirby, A. and Hamill, H. (1996) *A System for Evaluating Probation Practice.* Probation Studies Unit Report 1, Oxford: Centre for Criminological Research.

Robinson, G. (1999) 'Risk management and rehabilitation in the Probation Service: collision and collusion'. *Howard Journal* 38, 421-433.

Ross, R. R., Fabiano, E. A. and Ewles, C. D. (1988) 'Reasoning and rehabilitation'. *International Journal of Offender Therapy and Comparative Criminology,* 32, 29-35.

Taylor, R. (1999) *Predicting Reconvictions for Sexual and Violent Offences Using the Revised Offender Group Reconviction Scale.* Research Findings 104, London: Home Office.

Vennard, J. and Hedderman, C. (1999) 'Learning Lessons from Serious Incidents'. *VISTA* 5, 37-51.

Notes

RDS Publications

Requests for Publications

Copies of our publications and a list of those currently available may be obtained from:

Home Office
Research, Development and Statistics Directorate
Communications Development Unit
Room 201, Home Office
50 Queen Anne's Gate
London SW1H 9AT
Telephone: 020 7273 2084 (answerphone outside of office hours)
Facsimile: 020 7222 0211
E-mail: publications.rds@homeoffice.gsi.gov.uk

alternatively

why not visit the RDS web-site at
          Internet: http://www.homeoffice.gov.uk/rds/index.htm

where many of our publications are available to be read on screen or downloaded for printing.